W9-DGO-278

Acknowledgments

It's been said that writing is a mostly solitary effort, especially writing a book, and for the most part that's true. At the same time, it's rarely a singular effort, and there is no exception to that here. So my profound thanks and gratitude go out to the many who have helped me along the way, and there are many. Of special mention is my wife and life partner, Melody, whose patient listening, quiet encouragement, and constant support enabled me to write this book. Without her it would not have seen the light of day, which is true of so many of my dreams.

I also thank my dear friend and colleague Charles Lewis, whose wisdom, insight, friendship, and encouragement helped me see things in ways I would have otherwise missed. His knowledge, intuition, and sense of perspective are always right on.

There is certainly no bigger debt of gratitude than the one I owe to my editor, John Outler. His editorial skills, artistic sense, and dedication to this project have made this book infinitely more interesting and more readable. There is simply no one better at this work than John.

I would also be remiss in not thanking the many who helped me while I was at the University of Virginia. My experiences there transformed the way I work.

Finally, I thank all of the many workshop participants, coaching clients, and seminar attendees I have worked with over the years for opening themselves up to the hard work of becoming better leaders, and in so doing have given me the satisfaction and delight that make this work so worthwhile. Thank you all!

understanding

■

EXECUTIVE
PRESENCE

■

and how to make it
work for you

Paul Aldo, Ph.D.

Published by Gin Press, Norcross, Georgia

ISBN 978-0-9915721-1-3

Book design by John Outler

First Edition

gin press

■

**Understanding Executive Presence
and How to Make It Work for You**

■

Preface

The term "executive presence" might be new, but the behavior it describes is not. After all, truly exceptional leaders, those few with great executive presence, have always been with us. If you have had the good fortune of working with one, you undoubtedly remember the experience—the bearing, confidence, and command of the room, the clarity of speech and compelling vision, the thoughtfulness and accessibility that inspired you to be more motivated and self-confident. But where does executive presence come from and how do we cultivate it in ourselves? These are the questions I hear most often about executive presence—and this book is about the answers.

It might be tempting to think of the sudden and increasing focus on executive presence as just the next leadership fad. But there is something more—and more important—going on.

The growing interest in executive presence can be seen as a logical outgrowth of what we've been learning about leadership for the past several years. It was, after all, just 20 years ago that the groundbreaking "Must Read" Harvard Business Review articles on leadership were launched, changing the conversation from *whether* leadership could be taught to *how* to teach it. Executive presence is simply the next step in the evolution of this work. It extends what we know about leadership by augmenting the interpersonal skills needed to consistently garner the respect and influence that produce disproportionately positive results. It is the evolution of the complete leader.

The forces driving this interest in executive presence are the ones that have always driven interest in leadership training. The important difference now is a growing sense of urgency pushed by an ever more competitive business environment, one that demands more from all of us, every day. Organizations that win in the 21st century will be the ones that meet this demand, guided by leaders who are more complete and capable—leaders with executive presence— able to get more than their fair share of attention and discretionary effort from the people they lead.

CHAPTER ONE
Introduction

You probably picked this book up (or downloaded it) because you're interested in executive presence—yours or someone else's—and you're trying to see if there is something in the book that might be helpful. I'm almost certain you will find there is. Here's why.

Unlike other books on executive presence, this one plows new ground by addressing the two biggest stumbling blocks people have with executive presence: knowing what it is and learning what they can do to improve their expression of it. Not surprisingly, these are also the problems that cause most people to make only meager progress with their improvement efforts, no matter how hard they try.

The first problem is simply *defining* executive presence. Although we may sense powerful executive presence when we're around it, we typically can't put our finger on specifically what someone is doing to create those feelings in us. So what, exactly, are we evaluating when we make judgments about executive presence? The second problem is *knowing how* to improve our expression of executive presence. What concrete steps can we take that will make a real difference for us, and how do we stay true to ourselves while making these changes.

In Chapter Two we will define executive presence by moving beyond the simple "I know it when I see it" with a clear, objective definition that will help us think and talk about it much more productively. Without such a definition, and the vocabulary that goes with it, we can never get beyond vague behavioral generalities and the simple rote copying of behaviors we see in others. With this definition, we will also begin to establish the foundation for successful executive presence improvement efforts.

In Chapters Three through Five we will explore the Nine Expressive Dimensions of executive presence and some of the challenges people face in refining and balancing their expression. The Nine Expressive Dimensions are the things we all look to when making judgments about someone's executive presence, whether we know it or not. These nine dimensions provide a model that can help us more consciously analyze and shape our behavioral expression to noticeably improve our executive presence.

Building on the Nine Expressive Dimensions, in Chapter Five we will identify and discuss the behavioral tools we all have for creating executive presence, focusing on body language, vocal expression, and the way we structure and organize our messages. Chapter Six extends this with a discussion of executive grooming and dress.

In Chapter Seven we'll explore the important but often challenging topic of creating and delivering good executive messages, building on the simple but powerful Message Architecture™ model introduced in Chapter Two. Used with discipline, this model can improve the power and influence of our messages. Finally, we'll cover next steps in Chapter Nine, where we talk about getting actionable feedback from others and review detailed guidance for creating your plan, based on samples built around the four characters you are about to meet.

In this book I've sought to make improving your executive presence an approachable and achievable goal, but there's no getting around the fact that there may be some challenges along the way. To make the journey a little easier—and more enjoyable—I've invited four characters to accompany us. They will help illustrate some of the important concepts of executive presence through real-life scenarios and challenges that will culminate in actionable plans at the end of the book. I hope their unique personalities, aspirations, and paths will provide helpful touch points for you as we journey to greater executive presence.

Let me introduce Diane, Andrew, Melissa, and Blake. Although in different stages of their careers, they share a common goal. They all want to get into the executive suite—and stay there!

Diane

Diane is a hard charging, mid-career, 38-year-old. Since finishing her MBA at a top business school 10 years ago, she's had nothing but success. What people love most about her is her ability to make decisions and deliver results. She's energetic, engaged and focused on getting things done.

Diane takes a lot of pride in her leadership style and has always believed it would serve her well in her climb to the executive suite. And so far it has. But things hit a speed bump last week when Diane found out she was not going to get the vice president's job she was sure she had a lock on. Once she got over the initial shock, she sat down with her boss, Ben, to have a candid talk about it.

Ben told Diane that although everyone loved her results and thought she was doing a great job overall, some concerns with her leadership style had surfaced during the vetting process. Somewhere along the way, Diane had gotten the reputation of being too blunt at times and a little self-absorbed. The gist of it was that while Diane was usually seen as a great leader, she could turn inward and become autocratic when the chips were down. When that happened she would stop listening and become cynical, dismissing the suggestions of others with flippant remarks. The reports made the executive committee uncomfortable and they began to question how she would handle herself on a larger stage. They concluded that she needed more time to iron out some wrinkles before advancing further.

Andrew

Andrew is known for his patient, logical approach and for finishing what he starts. He's also known as a great team player, keeping everybody on board and working productively together. Not surprisingly, he has seen success in his career, which he characterizes as slow but steady progress up the corporate ladder. He's now a Senior Director, and has been for the last eight years. Although not overtly ambitious, Andrew has hopes of moving into the executive suite and has always thought he was on a path to do that. But now, in his late forties, he feels he's nearing a make-or-break point and thinks he might have somehow gotten stuck.

Andrew knows from past performance reviews the persistent advice about being a little more assertive in getting his ideas on the table and pushing them a little harder, showing a little more confidence and decisiveness. Maybe there's more to this than he thought. Reflecting on it now, he knows he hasn't made much progress, despite his best intentions. The potential for conflict when the moment arises always seems to hold him back. Could this be the tip of an iceberg that's a much bigger problem than he's been willing to admit?

Melissa

An engineer by training, Melissa has quickly risen through the ranks to her present (and new) position as plant manager. Along the way, she established a solid reputation for her dispassionate analytical style, data-centric approach, and calmness under pressure. This reputation, coupled with her excellent results, has made her a rising star, leading to her recent promotion.

As plant manager, Melissa is now responsible for taking the lead in providing operational updates to the executive committee as well as an occasional presentation to the board of directors. Although hardly new to the world of corporate presenting, Melissa has never been in the lead role in presenting to the company's senior leadership. Virtually all of her experience has, instead, been in support of a senior leader or in lower level, more operational settings.

After Melissa's last presentation to the executive committee, her third such update in three months, the company CEO took Melissa's boss aside and told him that he no longer wanted Melissa to do the operational updates. In the CEO's words, "Melissa may be a good plant manager, I'll give you that for now; but she doesn't seem to understand what's important in running this company. She doesn't get what we're trying to do here. There's no bigger picture; no sense of urgency about her. She needs to prioritize better and put more emphasis on execution. So for the time being, you give the operational updates and we'll see if we did the right thing in promoting her. It looks to me like she's in over her head. Maybe we're moving her along too fast."

Blake

Still in mid-career, Blake is already vice president of sales and marketing. He is full of energy and action and quick to get others involved to get things done. With his intuitive talent for spotting market trends and his articulate and persuasive approach, Blake seems to have the whole package. In fact, those in the know are sure he has a shot at the top spot in the not too distant future. Even Blake's hard-nosed, old school, CEO is impressed.

Of course, like most other successful corporate leaders, Blake still has developmental opportunities in rounding out his executive persona. He knows, for example, that in his zeal to get things done, he's not always an attentive listener. He doesn't always get the whole story before acting. Feedback from his team and a mentor has made that clear. He also knows that this same zeal can cause him to try to keep too many balls in the air at times, leading some to believe that he needs more discipline and focus in his approach if he wants to continue to advance.

While certainly not tone deaf to this feedback, Blake often asks himself how important it is it to spend much time on these issues. After all, it's not as though they're seriously in his way. And who's perfect anyhow?

If you're like most people, you'll see something of yourself in at least one of these characters, and some traits you'll recognize in friends and colleagues. Either way, our companions Diane, Andrew, Melissa, and Blake will help illuminate the challenges we all face along the journey to better executive presence.

Now let's get started by taking a look at exactly what executive presence is and why it's so important.

■

CHAPTER TWO

What Executive Presence Is and Why It's Important

■

W hen I ask people to define executive presence they always struggle with it. Instead of a definition, they usually give me a list of characteristics that conjure up what executive presence looks like to them. Or if they can't define it, they "know it when they see it." And that's okay if we're just going to talk about executive presence in a general way or share some observations about it. But if we're looking for a specific way to improve our own executive presence—or to help someone else improve theirs—then we need a more objective and practical definition. We need to be able to define executive presence in a way that helps us think more clearly about it and sets the stage for understanding exactly what those who have it are doing to create it.

What, for example, is the person who "commands the room" doing to command the room? What is a person who appears self-confident doing differently from one who does not? What can we pick up from watching others that would help us come across with more executive bearing? What we learn from these observations makes it possible for us to model the behaviors that create executive presence and incorporate them, or parts of them, into our own behavioral style.

So let's start by defining executive presence, and then we'll spend some time looking at why executive presence is so important to our effectiveness and career success. To drive this home we'll take a quick look at some research on the subject and briefly consider what traditional competency models have to say about the relationship between executive presence and leadership effectiveness.

Seeing Executive Presence as Behavior

Executive presence is a persona that we project to others through our behavior. It is the outcome of how we act (the way we stand and move, our body image, what we say, how we say it) and the way others interpret and respond to our actions. So the more executive presence we would like others to observe in us, the more we must behave in ways that project an executive persona. Seeing executive presence this way—as behavior—is a big step toward making it less mysterious by making it more tangible. Once we see executive presence as behavior, we can begin to understand, and control, the specific things we are doing to project it. For example, is there something in our tone of voice, vocal inflection, or pace of speech that suggests to others we look or sound like a good leader? Is there something about the way we make eye contact, walk into a room, or shake hands that gives people the impression we are confident and secure? Thinking of executive presence as behavioral expression, rather than innate qualities of personality, paves the way for learning how to identify and model the behaviors we want to project. And as we will see, most of what we're talking about is subtle. It's about the seemingly little things we do when we're with others that they, in turn, use to make very big judgments about us.

To help illustrate the behavioral foundation of executive presence, look at the two pictures below and note your reactions.

What do you see in these pictures?

Picture A   Picture B

What most people say about Picture A are things like "he's happy, he's having a good day, he likes what he just heard." About Picture B we usually hear "he's unhappy, he's angry, he's mean, I don't like him." While these observations may or may not reflect the underlying reality (after all, we can't see inside them to know how they really feel), what's important is that we formed our impressions inferentially, based solely on trying to make sense out of the behaviors in the pictures.

This is critical, since behavior is our common social language, both for projecting ourselves and for evaluating others. By keeping our attention on behavior we stay attuned to the things people use to make sense of us, and those things are always behavioral. Although we typically respond to others in terms of what we believe they think and feel, we must remember it is only our belief, based solely on observing their behavior. We assume the behavior maps to certain thoughts and feelings, but those are just our assumptions and they are not always correct. We will spend more time with this in Chapter Six.

Establishing Our Executive Presence

The process of inference and attribution we use in forming opinions about the people in the pictures is exactly how we make judgments about executive presence. The attribution of good or bad executive presence is based solely and simply upon others' interpretations of our behavior. If our appearance, speech, and body language are seen by others to project executive presence, they will attribute it to us. If we behave in ways others interpret as not-so-executive-like, they will see us as lacking executive presence. So the key is to always get the behavior right, while managing the underlying emotions.

But What Are the Right Behaviors?

So how do we know which behaviors are the right ones? Of the thousands of behaviors we observe every day, how do we isolate those few that will most improve our executive presence? Simply put, how do we figure out what to do and how best to do it?

To answer these questions I set out to identify those few behaviors that differentiated the "fast trackers" from everyone else. I started by observing and discussing hundreds of performance reviews and promotional decisions in a number of different organizations. I also developed and collated key insights from my coaching clients and Executive Presence workshop participants.

■

Who's Hot and Who's Not: What the Research Shows

In my research on performance reviews I wanted to understand why some people were seen by their organizations as "high potentials," slated for rapid career advancement, while the rest were not. What were the high potentials doing that set them apart and how often did organizations notice and act on these differences?

To help focus my observations and sharpen the analysis, I used three specific questions:

1. What behavioral expressions do people most often use to decide whether or not someone has good executive presence?
2. How do executive presence behavioral expressions influence workplace effectiveness and career success?
3. Are the behavioral expressions and criteria used to make judgments about executive presence universal?

Here's what I learned. There are nine categories of behavioral expression people evaluate when assessing executive presence. The same nine show up in executive presence evaluations over and over again. They were so consistent that I labeled them the Nine Expressive Dimensions, and organized them into three groups. The first three, *passion*, *poise*, and *self-confidence*, are about how we present ourselves; next, *candor*, *clarity*, and *openness* deal with how we communicate; and finally, *thoughtfulness*, *sincerity*, and *warmth* are about how we relate with others.[1]

My research showed that people with the best executive presence are skilled and balanced in projecting all nine dimensions. I also learned that people who are good at projecting the Nine Expressive Dimensions—those with executive presence—are seen as having

---

1 The term *expressive dimension* is used here to identify behavioral skills that result from effectively managing and expressing a combination of attributes, emotions, and behaviors. We will explore the Nine Expressive Dimensions in detail in Chapters Three through Five.

■

outstanding leadership ability and/or future leadership potential. It didn't matter how much content knowledge or job-specific skill they had. They were seen by their organizations as having something special and were typically identified early in their careers as highly promotable.

Finally, I learned that the Nine Expressive Dimensions are what people use to make judgments about executive presence regardless of where they work. City, state, and company affiliation make little difference. Although organizational culture has some effect—some organizations, for example, reward decisiveness more than collaboration, and vice versa—it doesn't change the importance of the Nine Expressive Dimensions as criteria for judging who possesses, or lacks, executive presence.[2] Organizations look for a skilled and balanced projection of all of them. The Nine Expressive Dimensions are what define executive presence.

Here are some things to note about the Dimensions. The first three are *personal*, "about us," and have to do with image and bearing, which is where most perceptions of executive presence start. Stand up straight, look people in the eye, and shake their hand firmly when you meet them. Wear clothes with lines and colors that flatter and contribute to a powerful persona. Always speak up and project commitment and confidence when talking with others. These things are critical to executive presence, but complete executive presence involves much more. That's where the other six dimensions come into play.

The three *communication* dimensions, for example, are used by people to make inferences about how we think. How smart and strategic are we? Do we have a larger vision and can we lay it out clearly and persuasively? Are we crisp and to the point when we speak?

---

2 Since most of the observations were made in the United States, the applicability of the model is uncertain in business cultures outside the U.S. However, limited observations made in Europe and Asia suggest the model is applicable, taking into consideration country-to-country differences in both expression and balance of the Nine Expressive Dimensions.

The Nine Expressive Dimensions

About Us:
The Personal Dimensions

Passion: Expressing focus and drive that show we are committed to what we say and do.

Poise: Projecting sophistication and composure that show we are comfortable in our surroundings and able to gracefully handle adversity.

Self-confidence: Displaying optimism and assurance that convince others we have the personal resources and resolve to lead.

About Our Messages:
The Communication Dimensions

Candor: Being honest and engaging with the world as it is, even when it is not as we would like it to be.

Clarity: Creating and delivering messages others see as crisp and compelling.

Openness: Projecting a willingness to consider other viewpoints without prejudging them.

About Our Relationships:
The Connection Dimensions

Sincerity: Expressing conviction in what we say and do.

Thoughtfulness: Showing interest in others and concern for them.

Warmth: Being physically and emotionally accessible.

The three *connection* dimensions, on the other hand, are about our relationships, how we engage with others. They are behavioral expressions that others observe to decide if we are accessible to them and willing to listen. Are we concerned with their agendas or only with our own? Are we easy to be approach and be with or do people feel uncomfortable around us? Do we keep our commitments and consider others when making requests?

In the next three chapters we will explore each of the Nine Expressive Dimensions in detail, looking at what each one means, how it is ideally expressed, what attributes and emotions underlie it, and the typical challenges people have with it. For now, just remember this: The Nine Expressive Dimensions are where we find our working definition of executive presence and the model for helping us improve.

EXECUTIVE PRESENCE IS DETERMINED BY OUR LEVEL OF SKILL AND BALANCE IN PROJECTING THE NINE EXPRESSIVE DIMENSIONS.

The Role of Executive Presence in Advancing Your Career

So what kind of effect can we expect executive presence to have on our careers? Simply put: decisive. Here's what I found when I compared the relative importance of executive presence skills to job-specific skills on promotional decision making: *Promotions into leadership positions were always positively influenced by executive presence.*

What this means is that candidates with executive presence skills advance sooner in their careers, and advance farther and faster than those without them. This is illustrated in the diagram at the top of the next page, where executive presence skill is plotted from high at the top to low at the bottom, and job-specific skill is plotted from low on the left to high on the right.

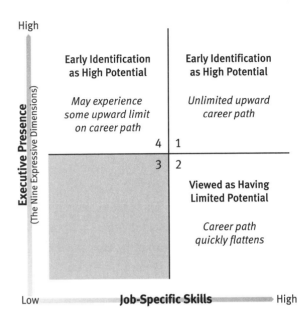

High

Executive Presence
(The Nine Expressive Dimensions)

Early Identification
as High Potential

*May experience
some upward limit
on career path*

Early Identification
as High Potential

*Unlimited upward
career path*

4 | 1

3 | 2

Viewed as Having
Limited Potential

*Career path
quickly flattens*

Low ————— Job-Specific Skills —————▶ High

Executive Presence and Career Advancement

To appreciate what this chart tells us, let's start with quadrant 1 in the upper right. These are people who have it all—high content knowledge and job-specific skills combined with executive presence. They are not only above average with the technical aspects of their jobs, they know how to speak clearly and confidently, get others on board with compelling messages, draw teams together to work for a common goal, inspire great loyalty, and manage themselves well through the stresses and strains of organizational life. As you might expect, they are almost always identified early in their careers as high-potential people and future leaders.

What might surprise you is upper-left quadrant 4. Although these people do not demonstrate any distinguishing content- or job-related expertise—in some cases they are even below the norm—they are also identified often and early in their careers as high-potential. Why? Because, like those in quadrant 1, they show an unusual ability to get above the details in presentations and conversations, articulate a vision, stay poised in the face of adversity, engage self-confidently with higher-ups, and understand and relate to the needs of team members. These are all behavioral skills from the Nine Expressive Dimensions and the skills successful organizations are always looking for in current and future leaders.

What's really troubling for most people and most organizations is lower-right quadrant 3. These people have plenty of content expertise and job-specific skill—they're often overflowing with it—but are short on executive presence. This means that they either do not express all of the Nine Expressive Dimensions well or do not balance their expression of them. Unfortunately, this is where most people find themselves. Think of the untapped potential, personal frustration, and potential job dissatisfaction represented here. Think also of the marginal return organizations are getting on their human capital investment, both in on-the-job effectiveness and leadership in the organization. This is why so many people being stuck in this quadrant is so troubling.

It is also unnecessary. Though people stuck here are often seen by their organizations as important contributors and solid citizens, they are also seen as not having much leadership or promotion potential. They are often labeled B players. Because the organization doesn't believe they have what it takes to move much beyond where they are, the opportunities offered to them are limited. But it doesn't have to be this way. Many people are in this quadrant simply because they don't believe executive presence is all that important, and/or they don't know how to develop it.

But how do we explain this? If executive presence is so important and the skills can be learned, why doesn't everyone learn them? What causes some people to develop these skills and others to miss out on them, either not being aware of them at all or believing they are unimportant? As we will see, the answer has a lot to do with differences in our behavioral styles and interests, which have a profound effect on what we pay attention to and learn.

If, for example, we think it is important to be good at selling our point of view and getting others to agree with us, we will likely spend time observing people who are good at persuasion. It's also a good bet that we will pick up some useful tips from our observations and model what we see. This is the informal learning process that helps us become more persuasive. On the other hand, if having factual knowledge and never being wrong about what we know are most important to us, we will focus far less on interpersonal subtleties of persuasion and far more on content and facts.

What Practice Reveals about the Power of the Nine Expressive Dimensions

The second line of my research that underscores the importance of executive presence comes from coaching clients and Executive Presence workshop participants. Their experiences provided me an important, up-close-and-personal look at the relationship between the things that cause careers to stall or derail—from the perspectives of bosses, subordinates, and colleagues—and the Nine Expressive Dimensions underlying executive presence.

What showed up over and over in my coaching was that a problem with one or more of the Nine Expressive Dimensions was the reason people were assigned a coach, were asked to find a coach, or were asked to sign up for an executive presence program.

The Nine Expressive Dimensions became the keys to clarifying both the problems and the potential solutions. They unlocked unrealized (trapped) potential by helping to clarify the generally vague offenses people were believed to be committing (lacking self-confidence, not seeing the big picture, alienating others, being self-centered—in other words, lacking *executive presence*) and the specific things they could do to remedy them. The Nine Expressive Dimensions enabled motivated and determined people to be clear about exactly what they needed to do to address their issues and how best to do it.

Not surprisingly, an important part of this clarification and modeling process involved 360 feedback, which is an essential tool for understanding how we come across to others behaviorally. This tool provided critical input, from bosses, direct reports, and peers, that revealed which of the Nine Expressive Dimensions were being modeled well and which were not. We are on the wrong side of our eyes to see this information for ourselves, so we must rely on others for it. Indeed, whether obtained informally or through structured tools, candid feedback from others is fundamentally important for defining our executive presence shortcomings and shaping the remedial actions needed to address them.

Executive Presence Is Composed of Essential Leadership Competencies

If you're still skeptical about executive presence being essential to great leadership and career success, think about this: all contemporary competency models contain competencies that are important pieces of what we are calling executive presence. Although the term "executive presence" is relatively new, many of the leadership competencies that make it up it are not. This is illustrated in the table on the next page, which maps some of the leadership competencies that appear on everyone's competency list to the Nine Expressive Dimensions of executive presence.[3]

---

3 The Lominger competencies are used for illustration since they represent the same leadership competencies found in all major competency models. They were taken from Michael Lombardo and Robert Eichinger's book: *FYI: A Guide for Development and Coaching*, Lominger International, 4th Edition, 2006.

Executive Presence Nine Expressive Dimensions	Leadership Competencies
Passion	Career Ambition Drive for Results Perseverance
Poise	Composure Comfort Around Higher Management Conflict Management Interpersonal Savvy Organizational Agility
Self-confidence	Action-Oriented Command Skills Dealing with Ambiguity Standing Alone
Candor	Informing Personal Disclosure Confronting Direct Reports
Clarity	Managing Vision and Purpose Presentation Skills Written Communications
Openness	Listening Creativity Peer Relationships
Sincerity	Ethics and Values Fairness to Direct Reports
Thoughtfulness	Compassion Caring About Direct Reports Patience
Warmth	Approachability and Humor

Also keep in mind that the Nine Expressive Dimensions work together, interdependently, to project something not called out in traditional competency models—*creating the feeling in others that we have what it takes, that we have everything required to be great leaders.* The Nine Expressive Dimensions are behaviors that, when projected with skill and balance, do that. They enable us to be more effective with others and to be perceived by others as having great leadership skill and potential.

Finally, each of the dimensions includes the traditional competencies, but as you will see in Chapters Three, Four, and Five, goes well beyond them.

Consistency in Projecting Executive Presence

Before looking more closely at the Nine Expressive Dimensions and how executive presence is created, let's discuss the importance of consistency. It is easy to fall into the trap of believing that executive presence is situational, that it can be turned on or off as the occasion demands. This, however, is almost impossible to do, and we shouldn't do it even if we believe we can. That's because *improving executive presence skills involves changing behavior, and changing behavior is difficult.* It requires discipline, patience, and practice. Only consistent effort that is "always on" will build the critical momentum behind new behaviors that will keep them from succumbing to the inertial drag of old familiar habits.

Consistency is also important because we are *always on stage.* We are always making impressions and being evaluated, every day, in every context. These evaluations are a fact of life. They happen whenever people get together—in meetings, presentations, and informal conversations. It's part of being human and how we get to know one another. But at work, the impressions we leave and the sense others make of them have important career consequences. They form our organizational reputation, which, above all, determines the opportunities available to us and whether we are seen as right for them.

It is tempting to think this is the province of formal performance management, but in fact it is your organizational reputation that opens and closes your career doors, especially when it comes to leadership. And when others offer or withhold those leadership opportunities, it is based on how they have evaluated your projection of the Nine Expressive Dimensions that constitute your executive presence.

■

What Executive Presence Is and Why It's Important

Seeing Executive Presence as Behavior

Executive presence is a persona that we project to others through our behavior. It is the outcome of how we act (the way we stand and move, our body image, what we say, how we say it) and the way others interpret and respond to our actions.

Establishing Our Executive Presence

The attribution of good or bad executive presence is based solely and simply upon others' interpretations of our behavior. The key is to always get the behavior right, while managing the underlying emotions.

What Are the Right Behaviors?

There are nine categories of behavioral expression that people evaluate when assessing executive presence: Passion, Poise, and Self-confidence—*About Us*; Candor, Clarity, and Openness—*About Our Messages*; Sincerity, Thoughtfulness, and Warmth—*About Our Relationships*. Executive presence is determined by our level of skill and balance in projecting these *Nine Expressive Dimensions*.

Research Reveals the Power of the Nine Expressive Dimensions

The Nine Expressive Dimensions are the keys to clarifying the problems people have with executive presence and their potential solutions. Understanding them enables motivated and determined people to be clear about exactly what they need to address and how.

Executive Presence and Career Advancement

Candidates with executive presence skills advance sooner in their careers and advance farther and faster than those without them.

The Need for Consistency in Projecting Executive Presence

Executive presence cannot be turned on or off as the occasion demands. Even if we could we should not because: 1) Improving executive presence involves changing behavioral habits, which requires discipline, patience, and constant practice. 2) We are always on stage being evaluated by others, which is the basis of our organizational reputation. Consistency is critical to those evaluations.

■

■

CHAPTER THREE

About Us: Passion, Poise, Self-confidence

■

In the next three chapters we'll take a close look at the Nine Expressive Dimensions that define executive presence. Along the way we'll stay in touch with our travel companions—Melissa, Blake, Andrew, and Diane—and use their stories to illustrate some of the typical challenges people face when expressing the Dimensions. We'll start by talking *about us* and examine the passion, poise, and self-confidence others expect us to show as leaders. In Chapter Four we'll talk about candor, clarity, and openness, the qualities people look for in *our messages*. Finally, in Chapter Five we will explore the thoughtfulness, sincerity, and warmth we show in *our relationships*.

As we explore the Nine Expressive Dimensions, it is important to remember that they are interrelated. A problem with one can sometimes appear to be, or even cause, a problem with one or more of the others. As a result, when we fix one problem we often fix other problems associated with it. The trick is to find the right one (or ones) to work on, which is what we will spend our time with in Chapter Nine, where we focus on creating our executive presence development plans.

The First Dimension: Passion

Passion is the expression of energy. It fuels the focus and drive that show people we are committed to what we are saying and doing, and gives others confidence that we are engaged for the long haul, come what may.

Passion is a trait common to all great leaders, but it doesn't magically appear once we attain a leadership role. It is something we cultivate long before in the day-to-day work we do. It's also one of the qualities organizations look for at every level when identifying future leaders.

This is nicely illustrated with a little humor in the movie *The Devil Wears Prada*. After a most unlikely candidate gets a plum job in the fashion industry, she finds it impossible to please her boss. Her smarts and hard work just aren't enough and she never seems to measure up. Her transformational moment comes when she realizes she knows nothing about the fashion industry and feels no passion for it. She is a complete outsider treating the job as a way to pay the rent. Once she begins to respect the industry and decides to engage by dressing the part and fully embracing the role, her career prospects—and her confidence—change dramatically.

It's tempting to think of this as "just a movie" and far from real life, but in this case real life is a lot like the movie. Carol Tome, Home Depot CFO and corporate star, finds that passion is among the most important leadership traits for surviving tough economic times. An article in the *Atlanta Journal Constitution* recounts advice Carol got from Arthur Blank, co-founder of Home Depot, when she started working for the company.

Although she brought a strict financial mindset to a company that was more enamored with square footage growth, Home Depot taught her some valuable lessons, too. "I remember, way back, Arthur asking me if I loved retail.... He told me, 'you can be a great finance person, but if you don't love the business, you're not going to be effective.' That really influenced me because I had to learn how to speak the language, not only from a financial perspective but from a merchant perspective." [4]

By all accounts, Carol learned and fell in love with the business, becoming a committed retail merchant from head to toe.

Characteristics of Passion

Passion is something we must feel. If it isn't real it will never be a sufficient source of energy and drive. When we're passionate we want to spend time and be engaged with the object of our passion. Jack Welch, for example, the revered business leader and CEO of GE for many years, was famously passionate about winning. Winning was his life blood and he was constantly engaged with finding new ways for GE to win every day. As Robert Slater writes in his book *Jack Welch and the GE Way*:

> He (Welch) could have resisted change. After all, as he likes to say, "GE today is a quality company. It has always been a quality company." So why not stand pat? Welch's answer? "We want to be more than that. We want to change the competitive landscape by not just being better than our competitors, but by taking quality to a whole new level. We want to make our quality so special, so valuable to our customers, so important to their success that our products become their only real value choice." [5]

---

4 *Atlanta Journal Constitution*, June 17, 2007.
5 *Jack Welch and the GE Way*, by Robert Slater, McGraw-Hill, 1999. p. 25. It is worth noting that one of Welch's books after retiring from GE was titled *Winning*.

To be truly successful we must bring passion to our work and embrace what really turns us on about our business. Passion makes us want to engage, and produces a different mindset and level of capability than what we get from simply doing the job at hand. We care more, notice more, and take more action—usually more quickly and more decisively. Passionate engagement focuses our mind so acutely that we think creatively at both the conscious and unconscious levels. The result is that we often surprise ourselves with seemingly spontaneous solutions to problems or with great ideas, when in fact these creative solutions have been long and silently nurtured by a passionate light we could never fully dim.

Expressing Passion

Passionate engagement is projected through very specific behaviors we look for when making judgments about how committed people are to what they do. Passion causes us to communicate with energy and excitement, and to speak with animation and intensity. Our level of involvement is infectious and we will always promote the object of our passionate focus to anyone willing to lend an ear.

What's more, passion breeds ownership and a striving for perfection that leaves little to chance. Be it an object, a concept, a practice, or a principle—a person, place, or thing—passion fuels a tenacious drive to learn as much as we can, to validate that learning, and to share what we know with the world. We can see, hear, and even feel this kind of passion in others, and it's pretty hard to fake.

Challenges with Passion

For *Melissa*, projecting passion gets "lost in the details." Before her promotion to her new leadership role, she had built her career on dispassionate analysis and data-driven problem solving. She was in the habit of communicating results and recommendations in a calm, detached, and efficient way. Unfortunately, this is not a style that lends itself to motivating and inspiring others, or getting them on board with ideas and initiatives. In her new and expanded role, she needs to focus on the bigger picture and explain it to others simply and clearly, getting them motivated and on her side. But Melissa struggles with shifting gears and expressing the passion for her work that would enable her to lead effectively. This has caused the CEO and other members of the leadership team to assess her as they have. Her dispassionate leadership style detracts from her executive presence and, ultimately, is not what the CEO wants for his team. The result, of course, has been a step backward for Melissa.

Blake is a very different story. Naturally persuasive and articulate, with energy to burn, he leaves no doubt about what excites him or about his interest in getting others involved. His passion is contagious and his natural ability to instill enthusiasm and get others on board is one of the things he is most admired for. But when Blake is fully engaged, he often initiates too much and gets too enthusiastic. When this happens he loses focus and follow-through, creating mixed messages and confusion about his priorities. Like most high-energy, enthusiastic people, Blake has some challenges controlling his passion. This is the big knock on his leadership and it is now holding him back. For his part, Blake struggles to recognize the importance of this challenge.

Andrew has never lacked for ideas and initiatives, but his failure to speak up and get his ideas out for discussion is a persistent challenge. He has, after all, been told repeatedly that to be a leader he needs to put ideas on the table and be an active part of the conversation. Still, when the moment comes he doesn't engage. Others interpret his apparent lack of engagement as a lack of passion and a reluctance to lead, and his career is beginning to suffer as a result.

Diane's challenge with passion is simply that she can be overwhelming. Settling is not an option for her; owning the initiative and the result is in her DNA what her reputation is built on. She makes suggestions and takes action with whatever force she feels the moment demands and has enjoyed a good deal of success along the way. Diane is not one to hold back, but her unbridled drive and ownership can sometimes be a little too much for others. As we learn more about Diane we'll see what can happen when we have too much of a good thing, and how important it is to balance our expression of the Nine Expressive Dimensions.

The Second Dimension: Poise

Poise is conveyed by projecting two different but related qualities: sophistication and composure. This is the dimension most often mentioned when someone is seen as *lacking* executive presence. We often hear things like, "she had all the brains and passion of a great leader, but she lacked poise."

The quality of sophistication derives from a comfortable belonging in any setting. In business this begins with simple social graces. At a minimum we should know how to dress to the occasion, make small talk, use the silverware, order food and wine, and speak clearly about topics that interest others. We should also have at least a passing knowledge of world culture, travel, and current events. Here's a real-life example:

> Three executives recently met to have dinner, accompanied by their spouses. Two of the three couples comfortably talked about business interests, hobbies, and travel, sharing likes and dislikes in a reciprocal way. The third executive, however, had trouble participating in the discussion. In addition to not having much knowledge or experience outside of his narrow business interests, he didn't understand the rules for reciprocity in conversation or how to be inoffensive with his comments. As a result he was either too silent or too critical and judgmental when he spoke. He came across as neither sophisticated nor charming. The next day the other two executives commented to one another about the third executive's lack of social grace, saying their spouses wondered how he had ever gotten as far as he had in his career.

Whether we like it or not, a simple lack of sophistication can overshadow many other strengths and seriously impair executive presence.

We show composure, the second characteristic of poise, when we demonstrate grace under fire and confidence and calm in handling turbulence and uncertainty. This quality was dramatically illustrated by Captain Chesley Sullenberger, when he and his crew landed their disabled aircraft on the Hudson River without serious injury to any of the 155 people on board. In repeated news reports Captain Sullenberger was characterized as the picture of poise as he calmly and skillfully solved the problem of where and how to land his suddenly powerless aircraft. Although business issues are rarely this dramatic, they can often challenge our poise. Leaders who maintain their poise, regardless of circumstance, are always seen to have more executive presence than those who do not. They retain the confidence of those around them by keeping everyone organized, focused, and protected.

Characteristics of Poise

Emotional maturity and self-control are essential components of poise. We may be composed when well rested and not under pressure, but we give it all away if we lose our cool under fire. We must be patient, thoughtful listeners and get the whole story before attacking a problem.

People who project poise possess a sophistication born of experience and preparation, so they are comfortable acting on an ever larger stage. They anticipate their developmental needs and seek the resources necessary to fulfill them. They actively *prepare* to be comfortable and self-assured in their surroundings by learning what is expected of them.

If, for example, we have had little exposure to top executives, our anxiety and discomfort will almost certainly show when we are asked to present to them, or worse, when we casually speak with them. We believe they are somehow different from us but are not sure exactly how. This is why it is so important to gain exposure to situations that can help us grow and develop the sophistication and self-assurance that confer poise. Making sure these experiences are properly digested and applied is one of the most important roles mentors and coaches can play in helping us improve. We'll talk more about the role of mentors and coaches in Chapter Eight.

Feeling comfortable and composed in our surroundings is especially important when dealing with organizational ambiguity. Taking the time to understand how culture, politics, personalities, and timing come together to shape organizational practices will make us better able to defuse tense situations with poise.

Expressing Poise

Vocally, we project poise through rhythmic, unhurried speech with relaxed inflection. We speak clearly, confidently, conversationally, and concisely, never fast or mechanically, and without word-like sounds such as *uh*, *umm*, and *you know*. We intentionally pause for emphasis without stuttering, stumbling, or filler words, speech habits that usually betray an underlying discomfort with a role or situation, and possible problems with emotional self-control. People with poise appear knowledgeable and articulate, never jumping on others or to conclusions. They speak to *all* others as equals, never arrogant, condescending, or overly anxious to please.

Physically, we express poise with relaxed eye contact, good posture, and appropriate grooming and dress. When eye contact is minimal, tentative, or tense, poise suffers, as it does when posture is rigid or slouched. A person with poise dresses appropriate to the role and occasion, and acts as an equal partner in social encounters, projecting comfort with whatever role they are playing.

Challenges with Poise

This brings us back to *Diane*, who is so passionate about delivering results that she sometimes loses her composure when things don't go her way. Her clear vision of what she wants and her ownership of task and time line often blind her to the input of those around her. When this happens her passion takes over. But executive presence requires both skill and balance across all Nine Expressive Dimensions. When one dominates, one or more of the others suffers.

For Diane, the challenge of balancing passion with poise has caused the executive team to hold her back, hoping that she will learn to balance her drive with a wider-angle, more collaborative (poised) view of her path to accomplishment.

Andrew's struggle with poise comes from a wholly different place. Because of his discomfort with being the center of attention and his desire to not offend, he often appears tentative and overly accommodating. He keeps his voice down, agrees too quickly, and rarely offers contrary opinions or stands his ground. His submissive body language reinforces these behaviors, projecting a lack of social equality in the way he unwittingly clasps and wrings hands, slightly hunches his shoulders, and avoids eye contact, as if he's trying to disappear.

None of this has gone unnoticed by Andrew's boss or the leadership team, and his behavior is raising important questions about his self-confidence. More and more, the performance reviews and advice Andrew receives are focused on how he is not projecting the comfort with his position that is expected for those playing senior leadership roles.

The Third Dimension: Self-confidence

When we're self-confident we project an optimism and assurance that convinces others we have the strength, personal resources, and resolve to initiate and to lead. We show self-confidence when we are positive, energetic and action-oriented in moving toward a goal, and when we are curious and direct in dealing with issues and concerns.

We also show self-confidence when we take the reins of leadership. Self-confident people are natural leaders. In addition to feeling comfortable assuming personal responsibility for championing initiatives and driving outcomes, self-confident people are not intimidated by taking unpopular stands or by the uncertainty and risk that accompany executive decision making. They eagerly step up to challenges with a healthy but realistic optimism that they can succeed. And though they may not always get what they are after, they quickly bounce back and learn from their mistakes.

But true self-confidence is not bravado, aggressive boasting, or posturing, behaviors that often mask a *lack* of self-confidence. Nor is it about a center stage, spotlight-on-me, win-at-all-costs presence, which are other ways we can hide shaky feelings about our ability to succeed. It is having a balanced sense of who we are and a realistic sense of what we can do.

Seeing self-confidence this way also helps explain the special place it has among the Nine Expressive Dimensions. While it is only one of the nine dimensions that people use to make judgments about our executive presence, it is the only one that enables the full expression of several of the others. How can we be poised, for example, if we are not self-confident, given that poise requires that we project a relaxed sense of belonging and the ability to gracefully handle adversity? Without self-confidence how can we be candid, which requires flexibility in facing the world as it is, regardless of how threatening that might be, or open, which introduces the possibility that we might be wrong or that there might be better ideas than ours out there?

Characteristics of Self-confidence

Although self-confidence can be expressed in different ways, the common denominator is good self-esteem. Since self-esteem under-lies self-confidence, which is so critical to executive presence, let's spend some time with it.

Self-esteem is how we feel about ourselves. Good self-esteem is feeling good about ourselves in our relationships, achievements, purpose, and potential. And we can feel good about ourselves even when we're not perfect, or perfectly comfortable. This enables us to be proactive, feeling powerful and in control.

Poor self-esteem, on the other hand, causes us to feel powerless and out of control. We blame others for setbacks and feel like vic-tims, unable to influence the course of events. Under pressure we often withdraw and may become anxious and resentful. We become pessimistic about possibilities and can't bounce back from disap-pointments.

That is not to say that self-esteem is constant. Most of us will feel some variation in it from time to time, depending on our mood and immediate situation. But generally speaking, people with high self-esteem tend to feel pretty good about themselves and those with low self-esteem do not.

One of the key challenges to self-esteem in organizations is po-sition power. This is because we tend to closely associate position power with self-worth, and usually unconsciously. We may know in our hearts that position power and self-worth are not related, but then act as if they are. The general feeling is that those who are levels above us in the organization must somehow be better than we are, especially if they are beyond our reach. After all, they have more power, make more important decisions, have more visibility, get more notice, and make more money than we do (usually much more), so they must have something we don't have. They do: different jobs. But if we allow the position power associated with different jobs to influence our self-esteem, it will show in our executive presence. We will appear too deferential and subservient, failing to project self-confidence around the very people who most need to see it.

Expressing Self-confidence

Projecting self-confidence begins with eye contact. Making eye contact is the first thing confident people do to establish equality in their relationships. Avoiding eye contact telegraphs uncertainty about ourselves and causes other to wonder if we lack the confidence to engage as equals.

Good posture also projects self-confidence. To appear confident, stand up straight but relaxed, shoulders back and head high. An excellent physical expression of self-confidence is a good handshake. When gently firm and extended proactively, by both men and women, it makes a powerful statement. Women sometimes miss this opportunity to project self-confidence by waiting for men to initiate a handshake.

When speaking, project confidence with short, direct statements, good vocal inflection, and moderate volume. Don't beat around the bush, back into your words, speak haltingly, or ramble—and never speak fast. Speaking fast quickly erodes executive presence by trivializing your messages. When you have something important to say, say it as clearly and powerfully as possible, using vocal inflection, rhythm, and pauses. Speaking fast forecloses this opportunity, making your messages seem small and unimportant. More importantly, it makes *you* seem small and unimportant since your audiences do not separate you from what you say and how you say it.

In her excellent book, *Confidence*, Rosabeth Moss Kanter contrasts the projection of confidence through the very different receptions given an Estée Lauder delegation by Kmart and Target.

The Target building was bright, clean, and colorful. Senior executives were on hand to greet the Lauder delegation. People were welcoming, enthusiastic, and well prepared. The Target team members introduced themselves by describing their roles and points of pride in their work...

Kmart headquarters was a forbidding fortress, austere outside, dirty and disheveled inside. A receptionist escorted the Lauder group to a dark conference room that held "two faceless people who looked depressed..."

The contrast was clear as each company sent signals about where it was heading. Target was on a winning streak, and the Target team's confidence helped them establish a relationship with a high-prestige supplier.... For the lethargic Kmart staff, failure was a self-fulfilling prophecy. By acting like losers in front of a supplier, they lost. Kmart declared bankruptcy in 2002. "Everything you do sends a message," Wagner (then vice-chairman of Estée Lauder) liked to say.[6]

---

6 *Confidence*, by Rosabeth Moss Kanter, Crown Business, New York, NY, 2004. p. 11–12

Challenges with Self-confidence

As you might expect, projecting self-confidence is another challenge for *Andrew*. His lack of eye contact, submissive posture, reluctance to speak up, low vocal volume, and apologetic style have led others to the unsurprising conclusion that he lacks the self-confidence needed to make it at the next level.

None of this diminishes the great job Andrew is doing today, which everyone acknowledges and appreciates. It is his future in a larger leadership role that is seen as limited, with the general conclusion that Andrew is probably where he should be in the organization.

For her part, *Diane* certainly shows no lack of self-confidence, which she projects both physically and vocally. At her best, she is the model of a confident leader and she is widely admired for her confident leadership style. At times, though, she can be blunt, autocratic, even flippant, dismissing (and often offending) those she works with. This is what bothered the executive committee. When Diane's self-confidence tipped into over-confidence, she showed a lack of respect for others' views and a self-centeredness that closed her off to alternative ideas. The committee was rightly concerned about what would happen when Diane was under pressure. Would she be the expansive and self-confident role model she most often was, or the closed off, out of touch leader, too caught up with what *she* thought should happen?

■

About Us: Passion, Poise, Self-confidence

The First Dimension: **Passion**

Defined: Expressing focus and drive that show we are committed to what we say and do.

Characteristics: We must *feel* passion; it cannot be faked. To be truly successful we must bring passion to our work and embrace what really turns us on about our business.

Expression: Communicating with energy and excitement; speaking with animation and intensity. Ownership and a striving for perfection that leaves little to chance.

The Second Dimension: **Poise**

Defined: Projecting sophistication and composure that show we are comfortable in our surroundings and able to gracefully handle adversity.

Characteristics: Requires emotional maturity and self-control. We must be patient, thoughtful listeners and composed under pressure. Requires a sophistication born of experience, so we are comfortable acting on an ever larger stage. We must anticipate our developmental needs and find the resources to satisfy them.

Expression: Rhythmic, unhurried speech and relaxed vocal inflection. Speaking clearly, confidently, conversationally, and concisely—never fast or mechanically. Relaxed eye contact, good posture, and appropriate grooming and dress. Acting as equal partners in social encounters, comfortable with roles.

The Third Dimension: **Self-confidence**

Defined: Displaying optimism and assurance that convinces others we have the personal resources and resolve to lead.

Characteristics: Founded on good self-esteem: feeling good about ourselves in relationships, achievements, purpose, and potential, even when we're not perfect—or perfectly comfortable.

Expression: Eye contact, good posture, and a good handshake. Speaking with short direct statements, good vocal inflection, moderate vocal volume, with no unnecessary words or word-like sounds (*umm, ah,* etc.).

■

CHAPTER FOUR

About Our Messages:
Candor, Clarity, Openness

The three dimensions we'll explore in this chapter—candor, clarity, and openness—are about how we deal with information, verbally and emotionally. They are concerned with how we react to potentially threatening news, the clarity and persuasiveness of our communications, and how encouraging and open we are to what others have to say, especially when they disagree with us. These things are what others look to in our messages to decide whether or not we are self-confident and able to chart a course of action, get others on board with initiatives, and move things forward. How we handle information, whether we're talking or listening, is a cornerstone of our executive presence.

The Fourth Dimension: Candor

Candor is about being truthful, with ourselves and with others. When we project truthfulness, people see our willingness to confront the world as it is, even when it is not as we would like it to be. They see that we can honestly deal with bad news as well as good, regardless of how unpleasant the bad news might be.

Candor is important to our executive presence for two reasons. First, people use it to judge our trustworthiness. Are we sincerely interested in understanding what's going on, or are we more interested in protecting ourselves through shading, distortion, and denial? Second, our candor says something about our self-confidence as leaders. Do we really want to face the music and do what needs to be done, or are we more interested in pretending a situation is something different and easier to deal with than it is?

Being a candid leader takes courage and often demands much of us. It requires that we admit shortcomings we would rather not admit; take full responsibility for our actions, even when they don't put us in the most favorable light; and encourage disruptive change, though we might be criticized for doing it. Candor demands that we look for news that causes discomfort rather than focus exclusively on news that makes us feel good, regardless of the short-term cost. How much easier is it, when the truth is especially telling, to blame, defend, and deny, or just "shoot the messenger"? Such lack of candor must at least *seem* easier because we see it so often, though it's obviously contrary to good executive presence and long-term leadership success.

Sydney Finkelstein, in his well-researched and insightful book, *Why Smart Executives Fail*, devotes a full chapter[7] to problems in-

---

7 *Why Smart Executives Fail*, by Sidney Finkelstein, Portfolio, New York, NY, 2003. p. 177-180.

volving a lack of candor, documenting its pervasiveness, causes, and consequences for the companies he studied. Here are some all-too-common examples.

At microchip manufacturer Advanced Micro Devices (AMD), for example, employees were so careful to maintain a positive attitude when dealing with CEO Jerry Sanders that he never heard about the serious delays plaguing the manufacture of the company's crucial K5 chip.... "Everyone in the company knew the thing was in bad shape but Jerry..."

Unfortunately enough, the higher people are in the management hierarchy, the more they tend to supplement their perfectionism with blanket excuses, with CEOs usually being the worst of all. For example, in one organization we studied, the CEO spent the entire forty-five minute interview explaining all the reasons why others were to blame for the calamity that hit his company. Regulators, the government, and even other executives within the firm—all were responsible. No mention was made, however, of personal culpability.

When people are afraid to draw attention to unwelcome information it's a slippery slope to becoming involved in cover-ups.... In publicly traded companies, the desire to maintain stock prices reinforces the other tendencies to suppress any bad news that might otherwise interfere with a positive outlook. For example, when Boston Market was under fire a few years back, the majority owners fired the CEO Larry Zwain, to try to shift responsibility away from themselves and signal that their house was now in order. Unfortunately, Zwain was one of the few people at the top who really understood restaurant operations; after he took the fall there wasn't much left to stem the bleeding... and the company ended up in Chapter 11 not long afterwards.

In addition to illustrating the importance of candor, these examples show that it's a two-way street. When we accept and deal with the world as it is, we must also be willing to share our relevant views of it with others, especially when those views are not popular or prevailing. Although difficult and not without risk, candor requires that we do our best to communicate openly and honestly, but always tactfully and productively, so that others have the opportunity to see things as we do. This does not mean our views will prevail, but if we truly believe something needs to be put on the table, we must take responsibility for putting it there, difficult or not. Otherwise, we are guilty of the same lack of candor illustrated in the examples, and usually with the same tragic consequences.

Another challenge candor brings is that it does not allow us the freedom to pick and choose what we will be candid about. Candor requires that we be candid about everything, constantly facing the world realistically and being honest and forthcoming about what we see. This does not mean that we must talk about everything we see—there are certainly times we will not—but it does mean that we must be honest when we do talk, and honest with ourselves (about why) when we choose not to.

Here's a final example that illustrates the great positive benefits that come from being candid and willing to confront the world as it is.[8]

Ford CEO Alan Mulally recounts an episode that makes him certain Ford has broken unworkable old ways and is locked and loaded for the future.

In one of his Thursday management meetings, where managers are supposed to show color-coded charts: red for serious problems, yellow for lesser issues, green for all OK. "All the charts were green, and I know—we're going to lose $17 billion. I stopped the meeting and I said, 'Is there any-

8 *USA Today*, Wednesday, July 27, 2011, pg. 2B

thing that isn't going well? We're losing $17 billion.' Eye contact goes down to the ground."

"The next week," Mulally says, "here comes Mark (Fields, now president of Ford's North and South America operations), and the charts are all red. Everybody else's were green. I started to clap, and I said, 'that's great.'"

"I looked around the room and said, 'Is there anything we can do to help'" resolve problems Fields was having launching the Ford Edge.

A dam burst. Other managers started tossing out solutions to similar problems they'd had.

Even so, managers took two weeks to follow the Fields example. "Next week everybody still was green, (but two weeks later) the entire 320 charts (of all the managers) looked like a rainbow. Everybody knew it was safe" to ask for help.

"At that moment I knew, and everybody else knew, that we had a chance now. You can't manage a secret. It was all out in the open. And everybody was committed to helping everybody else."

Characteristics of Candor

It is easy to see that candor requires a good dose of self-confidence. To find and face the truth honestly, we must have confidence in our ability to deal with it, regardless of how difficult. Without confidence, candor becomes a hill too steep to climb. In cases where we've made mistakes, we simply won't have the fortitude to face the criticism and consequences that come with admitting them. In cases where the challenges are greater than anticipated, we aren't likely to have the wherewithal to do what needs to be done.

Remember, though, that real self-confidence is neither bravado nor aggressive confrontation. It comes from a healthy and balanced sense of who we are, and not confusing ourselves with our roles. With this sense of ourselves we have more flexibility in admitting mistakes, solving difficult problems, and learning from our experiences, positive or negative.

But confidence alone is not enough. A real desire to do the right thing must drive our commitment to ethical conduct and our concern for others and the organization—and provide the foundation for candor.

Expressing Candor

Candor is expressed with reasoned analysis, a measured pace of speech, thoughtful inflection, and pausing. It is the opposite of defensive and confrontational argument. It is always respectful and requires sensitive communication, taking into account the anxiety or fear we may be creating in others by identifying unpleasant truths. These nonverbal expressions of candor are important because they are instinctively taken as a sign that the speaker is being honest.

The more we argue, blame, defend, and deny when we speak, the less candid we will appear to others, who will immediately suspect we are hiding something behind the obfuscation, bluster, and emotion. Our reactions to political office holders when they are in blame, defend, and deny mode confirm this again and again, showing the kind of angry, expressive emotion we just don't trust.

When people are being candid with us we don't expect to see a lot of emotion. We expect, instead, to see them thinking about what they are saying, engaging collaboratively with us, and answering our questions directly. We also expect them to "walk the talk" and do what they say they are going to do. This is yet another sign—and an enormously important one—that they mean what they say and can be trusted to keep their commitments.

Challenges with Candor

Diane is not bashful when it comes to being direct with others and she is known for getting right to the point. But being direct is only one part of candor. Another is honesty about what we see, especially with ourselves, which is an occasional trouble spot for Diane. When she lets her often stressful world get to her, she sometimes substitutes her version of events for what's actually happening.

This was on display recently with her decision to invest in a new marketing strategy. Convinced that the new strategy was just what was needed, she led an impressive internal campaign that got most members of the leadership team on board. Though she had a few detractors who questioned the underlying assumptions and projected return, this lack of unanimity was hardly unusual. The strategy was adopted and appeared poised to pay off with some top line revenue growth shortly after implementation began. But then quarterly net income was missed and then missed again, signaling a problem somewhere. Rather than rethinking the strategy at this point, Diane blamed the shortfalls on a failure of execution.

Under pressure, Diane finally opened the strategy up for another look, uncovering some faulty assumptions and making the necessary adjustments. But by this time the personal damage to her was done, and not because of flaws in the strategy. It was the way Diane handled the need for correction. Her lack of honesty with herself about what she saw and her deaf ear to the suggestions of her detractors (which we will talk more about in the next section) led the senior leadership team to question her readiness for the next level.

Candor is a problem for *Andrew* for two reasons: his need to avoid confrontation and his fear of hurting feelings. Unlike Diane, who never shies from confrontation, Andrew almost always does. The possibility that a situation might get tense causes him to withdraw. His withdrawal might show up in physically avoiding some situations or in simply not putting his ideas on the table for consideration. This is compounded by his discomfort with being in the spotlight, which leaves the sharing of good ideas and bold moves to others. In part, it is Andrew's unwillingness to be in the fray that's causing concern about his future. Because of his failure to speak up in meetings and let others hear his ideas, he's generally seen as lacking self-confidence.

Andrew's problem with candor also makes itself felt when he must hold others accountable. Although he holds himself to a high standard and wants those who work for him to toe the line, he has trouble being as direct with them as he should, which he makes even more difficult by putting off hard conversations. The result is that Andrew is not seen as tough-minded enough to be successful in a more senior executive position.

The Fifth Dimension: Clarity

Clear communication means creating and delivering messages that are crisp, easy to understand, and compelling. It is straight talk that quickly engages others and holds their attention. Communicating with clarity makes the listener's job easy. But how do we do it?

There are two things vital to clear communication. The first has to do with the way we construct our messages, the second with our nonverbal behavior when delivering them. We'll look at both in detail in Chapter Eight. For now, just remember that communicating clearly is essential to good executive presence. After all, how many people can you think of with good executive presence who don't communicate clearly?

Communicating clearly is key to good executive presence not only because it makes understanding our perspectives and following our logic so easy. It is also important, and critically so, because of what others read into it. More than anything else, it is what people use to make judgments about both our cognitive skills and native intelligence, whether those judgments are right or wrong. People cannot see us think, they can only hear us speak. As a result, they take how we speak as a direct representation of how we think.

For example, if someone seems to be missing the big picture in the way he communicates, we're likely to jump to the conclusion that he's not a big picture thinker (rather than a big picture talker or writer). We see him as somehow lacking strategic perspective and vision. Similarly, when we have trouble following someone's logic because it rambles or is densely packed with detail, we once again are likely to jump to the conclusion that it's a thinking problem, not an issue with communication.

What we are doing in these situations (usually unconsciously) is confusing verbal skill with cognitive ability, often penalizing the speaker for lacking perspective or brainpower, when what they really lack is a trained capacity for good verbal expression. Of course, not everyone has the same capacity for "seeing the forest for the trees," but we must be careful not to confuse thinking ability with speaking ability. Shifting our focus from how *we think* people think about things to how *they speak* about them gives us something tangible to work with. Improving our ability to communicate big picture views is what we will address using the Message Architecture™ model detailed in Chapter Eight.

Characteristics of Clarity

Self-confidence plays a key role in helping us deliver our messages clearly. If we don't feel confident in our ability to speak, or equal to the people we are speaking with, they will know it. They will see it in our hesitancy, lack of vocal energy, mechanical style, and muddled delivery, marked by the all-too-familiar utterances *um, ah, and so*, etc. Practice is one of the surest ways to avoid these problems. Nothing can take the place of speaking out loud with good feedback to hone skills and build confidence for the real thing.

A second characteristic important to clarity is patience. When we are patient with ourselves and with others, we are willing to spend the time necessary to understand the needs and interests of our audiences and carefully develop messages that clearly address them. Impatience, on the other hand, causes us to rush and not attend to the little things that can make or break a message. What's more, creating clear messages is an iterative process that demands repetition and refinement over time to ensure the right issues have been addressed in the most lucid and powerful ways.

Practicing delivery also requires patience, since we must be satisfied that our ideas are convincing and transitions fluid, with all unnecessary words removed. Clarity demands that our messages be lucid, conversational, and compact.

Expressing Clarity

Message clarity starts with content that connects directly with audience interests and concerns. The clearest messages do this with a straightforward narrative that lets the listener immediately know what the speaker is talking about and why. The audience is never saddled with having to figure out what the message is about, where it is going, or why they are listening. Clear messages resonate.

The clearest messages also share common physical expressions in their delivery. The most important are delivery pace, vocal inflection, and supporting gestures. Clear speakers do not speak fast. They choose and speak their words carefully and thoughtfully. They have something important to say and take the time necessary to say it as clearly as they can. They vary the volume and pitch of their voices (vocal inflection), use rhythmic phrasing, and pause to drive points home. These are the things that make voices interesting and attractive to listen to while giving listeners time to digest what is being said. Gestures, when used well, also play an important supporting role in highlighting and adding emphasis to spoken phrases.

A strong start and finish are other important characteristics of clear speaking. A strong start gets the audience's attention and it gives the speaker confidence, helping to create a quick and natural engagement. When coupled with a strong finish that summarizes the most important things the audience can take away, the likelihood that a message will be memorable increases dramatically.

Finally, it is important that you speak *with* your audience, not *to* them. This is the difference between collaboration and lecturing. When you approach your audience collaboratively, speaking in a relaxed and conversational way, two good things happen. First, you are more attractive to them as a speaker (since no one wants a lecture), and second, removing unnecessary structure and formality simplifies your message, making it more intuitive and accessible.

Challenges with Clarity

Public speaking is not something *Melissa* enjoys or comes to naturally. Given her interest in data and analytics, she would much rather study problems and identify solutions than discuss what she has found with others who, more often than not, don't share her depth of knowledge or content interest. As a result, Melissa has never learned to develop resonant, audience-focused, action-oriented messages. Instead of quickly identifying and addressing the interests of her audience, she gets mired in detail without a cohesive vision or satisfying narrative. Melissa's CEO put so much weight on the importance of effective speaking that he not only took away her role—and privilege—of providing updates to the executive committee, he also began to question her suitability for the executive suite.

It might surprise you to learn that *Blake* has a clarity problem, since we know that he is a naturally articulate and persuasive speaker who enjoys an audience. Unfortunately, those traits alone are not a guarantee of clarity. In fact, Blake's challenge with clarity stems directly from his easy familiarity with speaking and his attraction to it.

For people like Blake the problem typically shows up when the energy and focus they get from engaging others meets the warm glow of the spotlight. This can breed too much spontaneity and cause rambling, with progressively less focus on the point being made. For Blake, this has resulted in consensus among his superiors that he needs more discipline and training. In spite of his sales and marketing success, he needs to learn to keep his messages sharp and focused when he's on stage, a frequent position for any leader.

The Sixth Dimension: Openness

Openness is a willingness to consider the views of others without prejudging them. It requires us to be thoughtful when considering ideas and beliefs, especially when they differ from our own. When we're open we don't let preconceptions cloud our judgment, and we don't jump to conclusions.

But being open requires a lot from us. First, we must be able to listen, and listen well, as Granville Toogood points out.[9]

> Good executives have an ear for listening. Even if they know the answers, they ask questions: "What do you think is the best approach?" "Do you think this idea makes sense?" "Are these the people we should be talking to?" "Do you see a better way?" "Have we left anything out?" Questions promote ownership of shared ideas, which, in turn, ratchets up performance through the pride of participation. Questions build teamwork by unlocking talent and ideas. Questions make us all think harder and deeper. Questions help us learn.

Thoughtful and active listening involves genuine curiosity, and satisfying that curiosity also requires openness. It's hard to imagine seriously entertaining the responses others have to our questions if we believe we already have all the answers. Smart executives know they don't and tune into what others are saying to get a more complete picture. Perhaps you've heard the quip, "never ask a question you don't already know the answer to." With a little modification to "... *think* you know the answer to...", this quip now describes a key quality of openness. Smart executives already have an answer in mind, but are open to the input of others to improve, or even change, that answer.

---

9 *The Articulate Executive in Action: How the Best Leaders Get Things Done*, by Granville Toogood, McGraw-Hill, 2005, p. 75.

In addition to curiosity and active listening, openness requires that we consciously separate the message from the person delivering it. Focusing on the person can bias our receptiveness to their messages, positively or negatively, through the way we react to them emotionally. When we positively connect with someone we are inclined to give their messages a positive bias. Without this connection we're likely to hear their messages more neutrally or even negatively. If you think this is just human nature, you're right, and that's precisely why we need to guard against it. It's just too easy to fall into the trap of accepting or rejecting ideas based more on who brought them to us than on the merits of the ideas themselves. This is not to say that trust should never influence our judgment, especially when that trust has been built over time. But when it does we must still be open to the pros and cons of what's being said without regard to who is saying it.

Our receptivity to messages can also be influenced by how imaginative or realistic we are in our thinking. Highly imaginative thinkers have a bias for creative ideas, so they look for and favor creative solutions, sometimes without regard for their practicality. The reverse applies with highly realistic thinkers, who can be biased in support of the tried and true. They will give extra weight to ideas they see as realistic and practical, and will never be accused of proposing ideas that can't be implemented—but they may miss better ideas that could provide more creative and productive solutions.

Characteristics of Openness

Like candor, the most important emotional characteristic supporting openness is self-confidence. When we feel confident and secure with ourselves we're able to openly consider views that differ from ours without feeling threatened or defensive. Instead, we can use differences to seek common ground with empathy and a sincere interest in win-win outcomes. Feeling confident and secure gives us the flexibility to integrate our interests with the interests of others and approach solutions collaboratively. It gives us the latitude to acknowledge that the ideas of others may be as good as our own— or even better.

As Alexander Hiam succinctly points out in *Mastering Business Negotiation*,[10] great leaders realize that, "By collaborating, you can redefine the problem so as to make more desirable outcomes possible. Why accept limits when you have a chance to redefine them?"

Expressing Openness

We express openness by listening patiently with appropriate body language, such as nodding acknowledgment and focusing on the speaker without distraction. We also show interest by asking questions that check for understanding and clarify views.

Being open means listening, thinking, and not being threatened by contrary opinions or attitudes. If we rush others, talk over them, or quickly move on to something else immediately after they finish speaking they will take it as a sign we are not really interested in their views or what they have to say.

We also signal openness with relaxed, attentive body language that suggests we are thinking about what others are saying and not responding automatically. There are moments of silence, a measured conversational pace, and pausing. When we listen openly we answer questions thoughtfully—even ones we've answered a hundred times.

Openness is also expressed through a ready willingness to share information in developing collaborative solutions. When we are open to possibilities there is an easy give-and-take in getting information on the table and figuring out how to best use it.

---

10 *Mastering Business Negotiation*, by Alexander Hiam and Roy Lewicki, New York, NY, John Wiley & Sons, 2006, p. 134.

Challenges with Openness

Diane's challenge with being open is not in the early stages of problem solving and initiative development, when she's very good at involving others and getting their thoughts on the table for discussion. Her difficulty starts once she has committed to a course of action and is an active and visible sponsor of it. That's when she can close off, as we saw in the last section on candor. And the more actively and visibly she has sponsored the initiative, the less open she tends to be. Her impatience and need to be right limit her willingness to explore or acknowledge the changing realities of the situation as implementation progresses. Instead of being open to the possible need for course correction, Diane tends to be defensive and closed off to potentially helpful input.

Melissa's issue with openness stems purely from the way she reacts to new ideas and initiatives, and is mostly due to the way she frames her concerns. By nature, Melissa has a talent for seeing what could go wrong, so when faced with innovation her knee jerk reaction is to focus on finding the problems. As a result she is often temporarily blind to the benefits of trying something new and comes late to seeing the bigger picture. Her talent for finding pitfalls is not a bad thing. After all it's always important to carefully examine new ideas with a view toward what might go wrong. But the way she talks about her concerns often sends the wrong message. Her persistent focus on what might go wrong leads others to conclude that she is antagonistic to anything that's not tried and true.

About Our Messages: Candor, Clarity, Openness

The Fourth Dimension: Candor

Defined: Being honest and engaging with the world as it is, even when it is not as we would like it to be.

Characteristics: Confidence in our ability to deal with what we are faced with, regardless of how difficult. The fortitude to face criticism and the consequences of admitting mistakes when we make them. We must want to do the right thing.

Expression: Reasoned analysis, a measured pace of speech, thoughtful inflection, and pausing. Always respectful. Sensitively communicated, taking into account the anxiety unpleasant truths may create in others.

The Fifth Dimension: Clarity

Defined: Creating and delivering messages others see as crisp and compelling.

Characteristics: Confidence in our ability to speak to the people we are with and feeling that we are equal to them. Requires patience, taking the time to understand the needs and interests of our audience, and crafting practiced messages that address those needs.

Expression: Straightforward narratives that connect with audience interests and express intent with minimal detail and words. Requires rhythmic delivery pace, good vocal inflection, and supporting gestures. *Never* speak fast. Connect with audiences by speaking with them, not to them.

The Sixth Dimension: Openness

Defined: Projecting a willingness to consider other viewpoints without prejudging them.

Characteristics: Like candor and clarity, requires self-confidence, which allows us to openly consider differing views without feeling threatened or defensive. Disagreements are not zero-sum games we must win at any cost.

Expression: Patient listening and appropriate body language, such as nodding acknowledgment and focusing eyes on the speaker without distraction. Willingness to share information in developing collaborative solutions, with an easy give-and-take in getting information on the table and figuring out how best to use it.

■

■

CHAPTER FIVE

About Our Relationships: Sincerity, Thoughtfulness, Warmth

■

The final three Dimensions—sincerity, thoughtfulness, and warmth—are about our relationships. They focus on how we engage and connect with others. Are we sincere in expressing our thoughts and convictions? Do we take the time to listen to what others are saying and thoughtfully consider their points of view? Are we approachable? People want leaders to care about them. They want to know they matter and will look for proof in the way they are treated. Leaders who fail to grasp this will, sooner or later, pay a steep price in the spirit, loyalty, and forgiveness of those who follow them. Sensitivity and skill with these three dimensions is often what sets the very best leaders apart from the rest.

The Seventh Dimension: Sincerity

We project sincerity when we show others that we believe in and mean what we say. Whether we are displaying the courage of our convictions, apologizing, rallying others to a cause, or simply expressing support—sincerity is never half-hearted and is always heart-felt. It is the opposite of simply "going through the motions."

Sincerity is important to executive presence because it shapes perceptions of believability. When we perceive leaders as sincere we take them more seriously. We consider what they have to say, even when we disagree. We listen more openly and less judgmentally. Sincerity's emotional power also plays a central role in shaping perceptions of integrity and character. Sincere behavior garners trust and alleviates the fear of ulterior motives or deception, just as insincere behavior breeds caution and suspicion—the opposite of trust. As leaders, sincerity plays a big role in establishing the trust, integrity, and character that are among our most important assets.

Another important attribute of sincerity is that it is not something we can turn on or off as the moment demands. It must be consistent and enduring for others to perceive it as genuine. We must, in other words, walk the talk. Failing to do so will quickly destroy any trust we have established. People need to know that we mean what we say—at all times and in every situation. Here's a great example from Stephen Covey.[11]

> I was in my office at home one afternoon writing, of all things, on the subject of patience. I could hear the boys running up and down the hall making loud banging noises, and I could feel my own patience beginning to wane.

---

11 *The Seven Habits of Highly Effective People*, by Stephen R. Covey, Simon & Schuster, New York, NY, Fireside edition, 1990, p. 198–199.

Suddenly, my son David started pounding on the bathroom door, yelling at the top of his lungs, "Let me in! Let me in!"

I rushed out of the office and spoke to him with great intensity. "David, do you have any idea how disturbing that is to me? Do you know how hard it is to try to concentrate and write creatively? Now, you go into your room and stay in there until you can behave yourself." So in he went, dejected, and shut the door.

As I turned around, I became aware of another problem. The boys had been playing tackle football in the four-foot-wide hallway, and one of them had been elbowed in the mouth. David, I discovered, had gone to the bathroom to get a wet towel for him. But his sister, Maria, who was taking a shower, wouldn't open the door.

When I realized that I had completely misinterpreted the situation and had overreacted, I immediately went in to apologize to David.

As I opened the door, the first thing he said to me was, "I won't forgive you."

"Well, why not, honey?" I replied. "Honestly, I didn't realize you were trying to help your brother. Why won't you forgive me?"

"Because you did the same thing last week," he replied. In other words, he was saying, "Dad, you're overdrawn, and you're not going to talk your way out of a problem you behaved yourself into."

Sincere apologies make deposits; repeated apologies interpreted as insincere make withdrawals. And the quality of the relationship reflects it.

It is one thing to make a mistake, and quite another thing not to admit it. People will forgive mistakes, because mistakes are usually of the mind, mistakes of judgment.

But people will not easily forgive mistakes of the heart, the ill intention, the bad motives, the prideful, justifying cover-up of the first mistake.

Characteristics of Sincerity

Three characteristics that are important to projecting sincerity in our relationships are emotional awareness, focus, and empathy.

Emotional awareness is important to sincerity because to be sincere, to really mean what we say, we must be in touch with our emotions. It's about transparency. We must know *what* we are feeling even if we don't know *why*. We must make the connection between what we say and how we feel about it to be emotionally aware and genuine.[12]

Undivided, focused attention is also essential. We must harness our energy and devote it to those we are engaging. If we appear distracted they will see us as insincere and uncaring. Focus means being present with others in the moment.

Empathy means having a sense of what others in a situation are feeling. If we expect others to perceive us as sincere and genuine when we engage with them we must be able to take their feelings into account, whether we share them or not.

Expressing Sincerity

Sincerity is conveyed gently, both physically and vocally. It is projected through nuanced expression that helps establish trust in a relationship. As with the other dimensions, steady eye contact is vital. However, with sincerity, eye contact is typically softened with eye inflection, or raising the eyebrows to signal personal engage-

---

12 This connection is also fundamental to emotional intelligence. See Daniel Goleman, *Working with Emotional Intelligence*, for an excellent and comprehensive discussion of this.

ment and focused attention. This is usually accompanied by slight, periodic up and down head movement, signaling affirmation or understanding to the speaker. If we want people to know we are being sincere with them, we must show them by being physically attentive to their interests and concerns, completely focused and undistracted by outside influences.

Vocally we project sincerity through soft inflection, a calm pace, and plenty of pausing. As with our body language, we are creating a foundation for trust in the relationship. There is nothing argumentative, authoritative, aggressive, or rushed in our vocal tone. Pausing, in particular, is important in signaling that we are listening thoughtfully.

Challenges with Sincerity

Sincerity is another area where *Blake* has a bit of an Achilles heel, not because he's emotionally insincere but because he sometimes has trouble showing sincerity behaviorally. His interest in engaging others and meeting new people get in the way, causing him to look like a bit of a gadfly at times. At gatherings, such as meet and greet events, his interaction can seem superficial. Instead of being present and in the moment with those around him, his eyes and attention often wander, causing those he's with to ask themselves how interested he really is in them.

The Eighth Dimension: Thoughtfulness

Thoughtfulness is showing interest in others and concern for them by connecting beyond simple functional engagement. The thoughtful leader reaches out to create or deepen relationships on a more personal level. Although people sometimes question or push back on this, believing functional engagement at work is enough, it isn't. Whether we like to admit it or not, being recognized and cared about by others is important to all of us.

Although we work for money, most of us work for more. The "more" is the sense of self-worth we get from our workplace contribution. Leaders must be especially sensitive to this since being personally recognized by a respected leader can be one of our most important sources of esteem. When leaders go out of their way to thoughtfully recognize us for our efforts, they not only enhance their standing with us but garner lasting dividends in our talent, commitment, energy, and morale. This applies regardless of our position in the organizational hierarchy. As Michael Nichols so aptly points out, "We think of ourselves as individuals, but we are embedded in networks of relationships that define us and sustain us."[13]

A key to showing thoughtfulness in creating these more rewarding relationships is listening. But this means genuine, undistracted listening, the kind that requires us to put aside our own needs so that we can focus completely on the needs of those we are engaging. Here are some excerpts from Michael Nichols,' *The Lost Art of Listening: How Learning to Listen Can Improve Relationships*[14]:

> Effective listening requires attention, appreciation, and affirmation. You begin the process by tuning in to the other person, paying attention to what he has to say. Put no barri-

---

13 *The Lost Art of Listening: How Learning to Listen Can Improve Relationships*, by Michael P. Nichols, Ph.D., The Guilford Press, New York, NY, 1995.
14 Ibid. p. 109-111.

ers between you. Turn off the TV, put down the newspaper, ask the kids to play in the other room, shut the door to your office. Look directly at the speaker and concentrate on what she is trying to communicate.

Practice listening whenever your partner, family member, friend, or colleague speaks to you, with the sole intention of understanding what that person is trying to express. People need to talk—and be heard—to feel understood by and connected to you.

...But it isn't any particular comment or technique alone that will get someone to open up. It's taking a sincere interest in what the person has to say.

Listeners who pretend interest don't fool us for long— though they sometimes fool themselves. The automatic smile, the hit-and-run question, the restless look in their eyes when we start to talk—all these are giveaways to the fact that they're more interested in being taken for good listeners than in really hearing what we have to say. Real listening means setting all that aside. Good listeners don't act needy. They don't charm, flatter, provoke, or interrupt. None of that *look at me, listen to me, admire me, appreciate me*. None of that. They suspend the self and listen.

Characteristics of Thoughtfulness

The most important emotional characteristics supporting thoughtfulness are empathy, patience, and caring.

Empathy is important to thoughtfulness because it is our ability to put ourselves in the shoes of another and feel what they are feeling. We are able to read the subtle, nonverbal signals that others send and, if we are thoughtful, act on them. People who are not empathetic are often tone deaf to subtly expressed emotional needs and can miss important opportunities to personally connect with others.

Empathy alone, however, is not enough. By itself it does not guarantee thoughtfulness. An equally important characteristic is patience. Without patience, the most empathetic person can fail to be thoughtful. Patience gives us the ability to tune in with focused attention, not letting our own agenda distract us. We are sensitive to misunderstanding and disagreement and take the time to gather information and thoughtfully sort things out before making judgments. We also give others a chance to catch up with our thinking and proposed actions without rushing or pressuring them.

Caring is the final characteristic underlying thoughtfulness. Although we can be patient and empathetic, if we don't care about what others think and feel, it's unlikely we will act in thoughtful ways. When we care about people we are interested in them beyond their functional utility. We care about their aspirations, disappointments, goals, and interests. We want to make our contribution *through* them, so we are willing to listen and provide direction. We engage with them as people, not as things.

Expressing Thoughtfulness

When conversing, thoughtfulness is expressed gently, using the moderated gestures and soft eye contact that convey sincerity. Also like sincerity, vocal volume is moderated, with soft inflection. Because thoughtfulness requires complete attention to the needs of others, responses are measured and unhurried. This is a reflection of empathetic listening and is a hallmark of thoughtfulness.

Empathetic listening is also conveyed with attentive silence and clarifying questions. Clarifying questions, in particular, are important as they convey our intent to really understand the perspectives and feelings of another. To do this well, we must suspend judgment while listening and look for the whole story. We must be patient in not answering or offering advice until we understand the issues or interests from the perspective of the other person. This kind of listening almost always leads to probing and clarifying questions, unlike the "hit and run" listening mentioned earlier.

Another expression of thoughtfulness is keeping commitments. Nothing is more discouraging than a leader who doesn't follow through with a commitment to do something, especially something important to us. Intended or not, the message sent is that the leader's time is more valuable than ours. This is especially true when considering what the broken promises might have done to our schedule and plans. Thoughtfulness is even more subtly communicated through responsiveness. If we are only responsive (or most responsive) to someone when we want something, the subtle message is that we are more important than they are and that our time is more valuable than theirs.

Challenges with Thoughtfulness

Keeping commitments and being responsive to others are other issues *Blake* has with relationships. Although unintentional, his high energy level and interest in new projects make it easy for him to get too many balls in the air. When he does, he usually skimps on preparation and runs a little late, relying on his team to fill in the gaps. Those who work with him are well aware of this and have managed through it in the past. However, as Blake continues to expand his corporate role and take on more responsibility, cleaning up after him has become more difficult. Adding to the problem is Blake's situational listening, causing more than a little confusion at times around who does what, and when. The feedback about this is finally making its way up the chain, as is the apparent organizational confusion when executing some of his initiatives.

Andrew's issues with thoughtfulness are the opposite of Blake's. Where Blake moves too fast and doesn't pay enough attention to clarifying his initiatives and getting others on board with them, Andrew spends too much time making sure everyone agrees and is comfortable. As you might expect, this often results in delays and a loss of momentum. To Andrew's detriment, his care and caution are not interpreted as thoughtfulness. They're seen instead as a lack of energy and decisiveness, both by corporate leadership and by many of those on Andrew's own team. They see his problem as a need for better balance between airing differing opinions and moving forward decisively. To his credit, he's listening, but he still struggles with how to be more decisive while remaining thoughtful and supportive with his team and colleagues.

The Ninth Dimension: Warmth

Warmth, our final dimension, is about being accessible to others and being easy to be with. Warmth means removing barriers to engagement and inviting people in, showing our availability both through our physical presence and emotional openness.

The importance of warmth to executive presence is in the human qualities it projects. Leaders with personal warmth are seen as more human and more genuinely interested in the lives and well-being of those they lead. Their warmth also makes it easier for others to openly and honestly voice opinions and be less fearful of making mistakes. People around them aren't walking on eggs all the time.

Warmth also makes leaders more likable. And likability—contrary to a lot of popular business opinion—is important. Likable leaders are easier to relate to and follow; there is more good spirit and less grudging acceptance. There is also an extra buffer of forgiveness when things don't go exactly as planned. Even Jack Welch, who was not characterized as Mr. Warmth when he was running GE, seems to have understood this, at least with his top talent. "Losing an A (top talent rank) is a sin! Love'em, hug'em, kiss'em, don't lose them!" In other words, develop an emotional connection with them. Let them know that they are important and their contributions are valued.

Characteristics of Warmth

Supportiveness, inclusiveness, humor, and humility are all traits that define warmth. Working together, they facilitate a quick and easy emotional connection with others. Leaders who display these traits are perceived as people-oriented. Leaders who don't are often seen as aloof—not really tuned into the human side of the business.

Emotionally, warmth shares many characteristics with thoughtfulness. Patience is certainly one of them. To be warm and approachable we must be patient, taking time to recognize and engage others, soliciting their opinions and ideas. These are not hit-and-run encounters. They are focused and sincere, regardless of duration. Our full attention is on the other person, even if only for a few moments. Without that focus it is almost impossible to project warmth and approachability. Instead, we project ambivalence. A lack of patience is, in fact, one of the biggest reasons people are not perceived as warm and approachable, with so-called multi-tasking at the top of the list.

Another important characteristic underlying warmth and approachability is humor. This is not joke telling or backslapping humor, but a humor that helps us appreciate life's ironies and not take ourselves too seriously. Whether it is working to diminish our interpersonal intensity or simply getting us out of our shell, a little humor helps those around us relax and more easily engage.

Finally, humility is a characteristic common to approachable leaders. One big reason for this is that it helps offset the effects of ever-increasing position power as we move up the corporate ladder. Whether or not we realize it, others in the organization see us as more distant (and less approachable) simply because of the power differentials between us. Humility helps overcome this and puts us on a more even conversational footing. Maintaining a little humility also helps remind us that we're not the center of the universe, which naturally helps us be more supportive and inclusive.

Expressing Warmth

Warmth is projected through relaxed physical expression, with open positions, inflective eye contact (usually involving a slight arching of the eyebrows) and unhurried movements. But more than anything else, a genuine smile conveys warmth and approachability.

Initiating dialog is also key, especially as leaders, when our position power will naturally cause some people to hesitate to engage us in conversation. We must take the initiative by being consistently warm and approachable. Once a conversation is underway, it is equally important to stay thoughtfully focused on the other person or people.

Challenges with Warmth

Those who know *Melissa* well know that behind her matter-of-fact exterior is a person who cares about others and is sensitive to them. The problem others have is getting to know her well enough to know that. Her task-oriented, fact-forward style masks her warmth almost entirely. Always polite, respectful, and physically accessible, Melissa rarely shows or shares an emotional moment. With little inclination to engage in small talk or personal probing, she goes straight to the work at hand. It's only in reflection that she realizes the lack of a more personal side.

This was not much of a problem for Melissa early in her career, nor was it something she thought much about. Back then she was simply seen as a skilled, albeit aloof, technician, happy to be holed up in her office solving problems. Rising through the ranks, however, has changed the way others view her, with her lack of warmth becoming a real obstacle to developing important team and colleague relationships. Although she's finally coming to realize how important it is, she's not very confident in her ability to do anything about it.

About Our Relationships: Sincerity, Thoughtfulness, Warmth

The Seventh Dimension: Sincerity

Defined: Expressing conviction in what we say and do.

Characteristics: Emotional awareness is important to sincerity because to be sincere we must be in touch with our emotions. We must make the connection between what we are feeling and what we are saying. Sincerity requires focused, undivided attention and empathy, understanding how others are feeling and taking those feelings into account.

Expression: Conveyed gently, both physically and vocally, through nuanced expression that helps establish trust in relationships. Soft eye contact with eye inflection and slight periodic up and down head movement signal affirmation or understanding. Speak slowly with inflection and pausing; always listening.

The Eighth Dimension: Thoughtfulness

Defined: Showing interest in others and concern for them.

Characteristics: Supported by empathy, patience, and caring. We must be able to stand in the shoes of others, be patient with them without being distracted by our own agenda, and care about their aspirations, disappointments, goals, and interests.

Expression: Expressed gently when conversing, using moderated gestures, soft eye contact, undivided attention, and empathetic listening. Also expressed by being responsive and by keeping commitments.

The Ninth Dimension: Warmth

Defined: Being physically and emotionally accessible.

Characteristics: Marked by supportiveness, humor, and humility, working together to facilitate quick and easy emotional connections. To be warm and approachable we must also be patient, take time to recognize others, and solicit their opinions and ideas.

Expression: Relaxed physical expression, with open positions, inflective eye contact, and unhurried movements. Initiating dialog is key, especially as leaders. More than anything, a smile conveys warmth and approachability.

■

CHAPTER SIX

How We Create
Executive Presence

■

In prior chapters we saw that executive presence is behaviorally expressed. It is projected in how we behave and determined by how others interpret and respond to our behavior. In this chapter we'll take these ideas a step further and talk specifically about the tools we have for behavioral self-expression. We want to create an easier way to think about and analyze behavior and lay out a more practical approach to changing it.

Let's start by attending a meeting with Diane and Andrew.

Diane opens the discussion about an initiative Andrew recently proposed. She begins by making a very clear opening statement about her concerns with the proposal while making eye contact with each person in the room. Then, after very briefly and efficiently summarizing where the proposal stands, she makes some suggestions for what she believes should happen next and asks Andrew if he agrees. She does all of this in a supportive and non-confrontational way. Diane's voice is clear, well modulated, and loud enough for everyone in the room to hear. Her pace of speech is slow but rhythmic, with vocal inflection that conveys her sincere interest in ensuring that the initiative will be successful.

When Diane is finished, Andrew clears his throat and begins to address her suggestions. He avoids eye contact with anyone for longer than an instant, looking mostly at his notes and the conference table. His voice is soft and tentative with little inflection. And while he knows his content and has a firm grasp of the facts, his presentation begins to ramble. Others in the room start to ask themselves if he has enough drive and direction for the project. When he finally stops talking, no one is sure if he adequately addressed Diane's questions or, more importantly, if he even understands the broader context and purpose of the initiative he is responsible for.

What impressions do you think Diane and Andrew left with the other people in the room? Who do you think was identified as having the most leadership potential? Diane, of course. Her organized, clear, and proactive message won the day. Listeners took note of her physical expression, inflection, pace of speech, and the way her message was organized and on point. Her commanding nonverbal behavior, projected in both her body language and auditory self-expression—her executive presence—caused the people in the audience to place their bets with her.

Our Tools of Self-expression

Our discussion of nonverbal behavior so far has been broadly focused. Now it's time to get specific. How, exactly, do we produce the hundreds of unique, subtle, and complex nonverbal behaviors we try to make sense of everyday? It might surprise you to learn that we do it with a remarkably small number of tools. There are, in fact, only six: eyes, face, body, voice, the pace of our speech, and the architecture of our messages. These are our tools of self-expression and all of our behaviors are produced through the way we combine and use these six tools.

If this makes you think something must be missing, it's probably because you don't think about behavior this way. Most people don't. They think about it more holistically and less analytically, and almost always with inferences about the psychological state of the person being observed.

For example, when I first ask my Executive Presence workshop participants to analyze someone's behavior in a video clip, they invariably use words like mad, glad, sad, self-confident, self-conscious, or shy. It takes them a while to shift their focus to analyzing the behavioral details their inferences are based on, such as how the person is using his eyes, face, body, voice, the pacing of his speech, and the architecture of his message. But if we're serious about learning how to project ourselves more powerfully, this is exactly the level of behavioral detail we need to look at. We need to understand the basis for the conclusions that others are making about us and that we are making about them.

These conclusions are always made by evaluating how we use our tools of self-expression: our eyes, faces, bodies, voices, the pace of our speech, and the architecture of our messages. Let's look at each in more detail.

Eyes

It has been said that the eyes are the windows to the soul. Maybe that's why eye contact is so important and why we prefer face-to-face encounters when something big is at stake. We simply believe we can tell more about people when we look them in the eyes. So the first thing to remember about the eyes is to make eye contact when engaging others. Use a relaxed gaze (not an expressionless stare) that focuses on the eyes most of the time. When you avoid looking someone in the eyes, they are likely to assume something is amiss and question your behavior. Does she lack self-confidence, is he uncomfortable with us, is she being completely honest? These are the things people think about when you don't make eye contact. None of them are good.

Also be aware of how you use the muscles around your eyes. Subtle movement in these muscles can produce big changes in your expression, whether you mean to or not. Moving the eyebrows down one millimeter begins to form a mean stare. Moving them up one millimeter begins to form a questioning look. For an illustration, go back to the pictures on page 11 and note what the eyes alone tell you.

How you use your eyelids—the blink rate and how open or closed they are—also gets noticed. Blinking more than once every few seconds becomes noticeable to others. As your blink rate approaches one-per-second, you begin to appear nervous, stressed, or deceitful. On the other hand, blinking slowly and holding your eyelids closed for a second or two can make you seem bored, arrogant, or dismissive, especially if you lift your eyebrows slightly and look upward when opening your eyes. And it goes without saying that eye rolling is never a good idea.

To appear energetic, engaged, and in control, all hallmarks of good executive presence, make eye contact with a relaxed gaze, keep your eyes open, and use your eyebrows for inflection.

Face

Facial movements involve the way we use our mouths and cheeks, which is how we create our most important facial expression, a smile. A genuine smile does three things. It projects warmth, makes us approachable, and conveys a calm and collected demeanor. It is one of our most powerful forms of nonverbal communication.

For illustration go back again to the pictures on page 11. This time cover up the eyes and focus on the rest of the face. How does the smile in Picture A make you feel when you compare it to the stern expression in Picture B? The person in Picture A looks inviting and engaged, the person in Picture B looks anything but.

Smiling creates a more generous relationship. People like you more when you smile at them and you like them more when they smile at you. There is more room for flexibility and accommodation, with a greater willingness to consider positions and ideas that might at first be disagreeable. When you don't smile, others can take it as a sign that you are not interested in them as people. Instead of enhancing the chances of getting them on board with your ideas or integrated into your team, you may do just the opposite, regardless of your underlying intentions. This becomes more pronounced as you move up the corporate ladder and acquire more position power, a point that was recently brought home by a coaching client whose team was on the verge of mutiny. He began his turnaround with the simple act of smiling. By sincerely smiling at his team members when he saw them and then showing a personal interest in them, he paved the way for acceptance as their leader. They slowly began to see him as someone who cared about them and what they thought, and from these simple seeds relationships began to grow.

Of course, there are times when a smile is not appropriate, but when you are not smiling, be mindful of the signals your face can send. The furrowed brow of deep thought or concentration could be seen as a threat. And negative thoughts of any kind are likely to show on your face. The point is to be aware that, as a leader, people will be looking to your facial expressions more than ever for cues about your thoughts and disposition.

Body

Our bodies send messages principally through our posture and how we use our arms and legs. Look at the picture below.

What do you see? Does she look interested in a reasonable discussion or even open to one? The answer, obviously, is no. Why? Because of the signals she is sending with her body (compounded by the way she is using her eyes and face). Notice the tightly crossed arms and crossed legs, combined with the slightly tensed shoulders and upright posture pushed to the back of the chair. There is hardly anything more she could do to tell us to beware.

Just as your body language can signal being closed, angry, or defiant, it can also signal insecurity, nervousness, and low self-confidence. Hand wringing, a slumped posture, and limp handshakes do this. So be careful of the way you sit, stand, and use your arms and legs when you are with others. Always maintain good posture, look people in the eye when you talk with them, and initiate greetings with a firm handshake. Be ever conscious and careful of the signals you are sending.

Voice

Voice is the auditory part of our nonverbal behavior. Like body language, the sound and quality of the voice creates powerful meaning well beyond the words that are spoken. There are five vocal characteristics that do this: resonance, pitch, volume, inflection, and diction.

Resonance: Resonance is the vocal characteristic that makes a voice rich. Think of it as filling space. Although often associated with the authoritative reverberation of deep base tones, it is not limited only to those with deep voices. Higher pitched voices can be resonant as well. To get the most resonance out of your voice, whatever pitch it is, you must breathe properly when speaking. Breathing from your diaphragm and pushing air across your larynx will create more resonance in your voice. Why should you care about this? Because a fuller, more resonant voice is associated with authority. Fuller voices project confidence and self-assurance, regardless of pitch.

Pitch: Pitch involves variation from high to low tones. It is what makes our voices interesting. Speak in a monotone is speaking without variation in pitch. This is important because others interpret the absence of pitch as an absence of passion, energy, emotion, commitment, and caring. It's also boring. You will quickly lose your listeners if you speak in a monotone. In addition to vocal variation, pitch also involves the natural tone of the voice. Some of us have higher or lower pitched voices than others. Although there is research suggesting that lower pitched voices can convey more authority, the tone of the voice alone does not do this. Rather, authority is conveyed through the sum of all of our nonverbal behavior. General George Patton, for example, the epitome of authority and military bearing, had such a high pitched voice it almost squeaked. But no one ever accused him of lacking authority.

Volume: Volume is variation in sound intensity, from soft or quiet tones to loud ones. The two big problems with volume are not speaking loudly enough and fading out at the end of sentences. Both interfere with good executive presence. Not speaking loudly enough makes you appear less confident and minimizes the importance of what you are saying. Fading out at the end of sentences strains your listener's ability, and willingness, to stay tuned in. It's also irritating. If you have either of these problems, you will improve your executive presence by getting rid of them through disciplined attention and practice.

Inflection: Vocal inflection, which is produced by coupling volume and pitch, is the most important nonverbal signal we send. It's what we look to, more than anything else, to make judgments about others. Are they in a good or bad mood? Do they really care about what we think or are they just going through the motions? Are they respectful or condescending, confident or unsure? Listening to vocal inflection is the way we answer these questions and others like them. Remember this too: vocal inflection becomes even more important in the absence of other nonverbal cues. When you are on the telephone, for example, you are operating in a restricted environment. You can't see the other person. The only nonverbal cues are vocal, so you must rely almost exclusively on them to make your assessments. It is important to stay particularly attentive to your own vocal inflection in these situations since it's so easy to get lazy. Others may not be able to see you with their eyes, but you are "visible" to them through the emotion you convey with your voice. They may not see the eye roll or smirk, but they can almost always "hear" it, so be careful. A good technique when on the phone is to speak as if you were face-to-face; this will ensure that your nonverbals do not conflict with your message.

Diction: Diction is about word choice and pronunciation. Good diction results from using the right words for the occasion and pronouncing them correctly. This is important to your executive presence because others look to your diction to make inferences about your level of education, worldly experience, and particularly your sophistication. Poor diction creates the opposite impression. If you are unsure about your diction, make a recording of yourself speaking and see if you like the way it sounds. Playing it for a speaker you admire is also a great way to get valuable feedback. Recording yourself is an excellent and overlooked improvement tool that is both inexpensive and easy. Try it. You can use it to assess the other aspects of your voice as well.

Pace of Speech

There are two things to consider with the pace of your speech: speed and rhythm.

Speed: The simple rule with speed is *never speak fast—ever!* Violating this rule will always hurt your executive presence. There are several reasons why. First, speaking fast trivializes your message. It tells your audience that what you have to say is not important. If it were, you would take your time with it, emphasizing your most important points with vocal inflection and pauses. You would let your message sink in and give your audience time to think about it. Speaking fast limits your ability to do this in any meaningful way. Second, because your audience will not separate you from your message, speaking fast will make you look less like a leader and more like a technician or messenger. This is a sure way to diminish your executive presence, since leaders are rarely confused with technicians and messengers. Third, speaking fast limits your ability to introduce interest and drama into your speech. Changing cadence and pausing for emphasis do not work well when you are rushing through your message. The opportunity for variety and drama that speaking fast forecloses means that you will be less interesting to listen to. It also means that your messages will not get the attention you would like. The best leaders know this and do everything possible to be interesting and energizing. Finally, authority is conveyed through slower paced speech. Listen to powerful leaders and you will hear it. Although rhythmic, they are never rushed. What they have to say is too important for that.

Rhythm: Rhythm refers to the pace at which your voice moves across the syllables and words in your sentences. When coupled with vocal inflection it makes you sound more interesting and energetic, which attracts and holds audience attention. Rhythm is more difficult than speed because there are no simple rules for it. Speaking rhythmically and using pauses appropriately requires motivation, as well as practice and patience. You must really want to master it and be actively interested in how you sound to others. If not, it is unlikely you will spend the time analyzing how you sound today and practicing the changes that will help you improve tomorrow. Getting a feel for the rhythm of powerful speech also requires some trial and error. Since there is no real formula to use, improvement comes from speaking and listening, trying different things, and listening again. This is time well spent, however, and the payback to your executive presence will be well worth the effort.

Architecture of Our Messages

A well-architected message makes our ideas clear and convincing, alive and persuasive, inclusive and collaborative—and it separates extraordinary from ordinary speakers. The best speakers not only use the behavioral tools we've discussed for maximum effect, they also construct their messages to clearly and directly address audience concerns in a narrative framework that creates powerful results. Here is a preview of the Message Architecture™ method that we will discuss in detail in Chapter Eight.

1. **Say what you want:** You should be able to write down what you want from your message in a simple, unambiguous statement. Do not start creating your message until you have done this.

2. **List the hurdles:** You must understand the interests, concerns, and objections of your audience. You cannot sidestep or finesse these issues. If you try to, your audience will think that you either do not understand their interests (you are clueless) or that you cannot deal with them (you are irrelevant). In either case, your message will fail and you will lose.

3. **Lower the hurdles:** Create the main components of your message (your argument) by persuasively addressing *all* of the interests and concerns of your audience. Creatively construct your best evidence for each point you will address, then provide no more detail than absolutely necessary. And remember that *facts do not persuade!* Logical conclusions, artfully presented, do.

4. **Compose your message:** Keep your message interesting and memorable by finding its natural "story." Assemble the message elements in a way that makes the story flow and logically ties your arguments together. When your story is easy to tell and has a natural narrative quality, you are ready for the final step.

5. **Refine your message:** Review and edit your message for simplicity. Make it as straightforward as you can. Be sure your audience understands why they are there, what you want from them, and why it's a good deal for them, using simple words and short sentences. Do not stray from the elements that make up your story.

Connecting the Dots

Our focus so far has been on behavior and how others evaluate it. We've taken that approach because our behavior is the only thing about us others have access to. Our behavior is how they experience us. But we know that behavior isn't everything. We also have thoughts and feelings behind that behavior, which we discussed when exploring the Nine Expressive Dimensions. So how do these parts and pieces fit together when we're interacting with one another? The Interpersonal Presence Model illustrates this.

The Interpersonal Presence Model

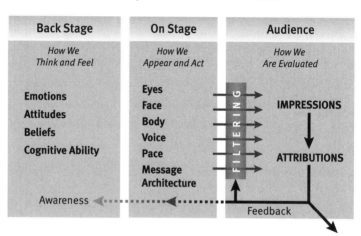

From left to right, the model connects: 1) who we are inside our skins, which is *back stage* and out of view of those we interact with; 2) how we project ourselves to others through our behavior, which is on stage and visible to everyone but us; and 3) how others "create" us in their minds by reacting to what they see and hear.

Let's take a closer look at what's going on in each stage.

Back Stage

Back stage is where we think and feel. It's where our thoughts, emotions, attitudes, beliefs, biases, prejudices, and knowledge reside. It is our internal life. When we're mad, sad, glad, happy, anxious, or confident, this is where we feel it. When we are preparing to have a difficult conversation with an employee, give a critical presentation to senior management, or have a heart-to-heart talk with the boss, everything we are thinking and feeling is here. Back stage is invisible to our audience, and only accessible to them through the ways it influences onstage behavior, and then only by inference.

On Stage

On stage is where we act with others. It's about our behavior, the way we use our eyes, faces, bodies, voices, the pace of our speech, and architecture of our messages to convey what we're thinking and feeling. It is how we project ourselves to other people, or try to hide from them what we are really thinking and feeling. On stage is where others see and hear that difficult conversation, critical presentation, or heart-to-heart with the boss. It is the visible us.

This does not mean that what we project to others when we are on stage will be accurately interpreted, or even that we will project ourselves accurately. But the more we are in touch with our own behavior and in control of our messages, the more likely we will be to accurately project our thoughts and feelings when we act.

Audience

Using the behavioral signals we send, our audiences evaluate our onstage behavior to come to conclusions about us. They decide what we mean and who we are, whether our signals to them are intentional or not.

This process starts as soon as people take notice of us, making their initial assessment based on our appearance alone when we are face-to-face. And the conclusions they draw from their initial impressions occur within the first few seconds of the encounter.

These impressions, however, are not without bias. They are filtered, based on a range of things, including what others have heard or read about us, what they believe we stand for, how our messages resonate with their own biases and beliefs, their accumulated impressions of us from previous encounters, their conclusions about us from discussions with other people, and the mood they happen to be in that day. All of these contribute to their conclusions about who we are and what we're "made of."

Filtering also explains why different people interpret the same nonverbal cues in different ways. A good example is the way we evaluate political candidates, a process where our emotional filters predominate. According to Drew Westen,[15] author of *The Political Brain*, the emotional appeal of a political candidate's message is the most important thing in determining how the message will be received by the electorate, though that very same electorate believes it is reacting logically. The reason we confuse logic and emotion in this way is that we tend to filter subconsciously. Even when we are aware of filtering (bias) we are likely to underestimate its extent. This is important to remember, as this sub- or semi-conscious filtering process also influences how we receive and interpret everyday messages from our bosses, colleagues, and those reporting to us, as well as how they interpret our messages to them. As a result, what was said and what was heard can often pass through surprisingly different filters.

Once our behavior has passed through the audience's filters, two important things happen that complete the encounter. First, they

---

15 Drew Westen is a psychologist drawing on research in psychology and cognitive neuroscience to make a convincing case for his perspective. See Drew Westen, *The Political Brain: The Role of Emotion in Deciding the Fate of a Nation*, New York: Public Affairs Publishers, 2007.

form, or reinforce, impressions of us. Second, they attribute characteristics to us based on those impressions. This is not a process of discovery; rather, it is how each member of our audience "creates" us. It's all made up. We're seen as smart or dumb, strong or weak, honest or untrustworthy based on how our audiences have made sense of our behavior. So what we feel on the inside matters little if it is not reflected through our words, gestures, actions, inflections, and tone—even dress. Behavior—what's on the outside—is all the audience has.

How We Create Executive Presence

Our Tools of Self-expression

Executive presence is created behaviorally, through the way we use our tools of self-expression: eyes, face, body, voice, the pace of our speech, and the architecture of our messages.

Non-auditory Tools: Eyes, Face, Body—the *body language* tools. We send powerful messages with eye contact (or avoiding it), facial movement (especially smiling), and posture. Through body language alone, others make important decisions about our emotional state, e.g., confident, happy, closed, angry, defiant, insecure, nervous.

Auditory Tools: Voice and Pace. The important parts of voice are resonance, inflection (combining pitch and volume), and diction. Pace of speech consists of the speed of our speech and the variation in rhythm as we move across words, sentences, and phrases. As with body language, voice and pace send powerful messages to others about us. A cardinal rule is never speak fast.

Message Architecture™: The Five Step Model

Step 1: Say what you want. What do you want you audience to think or do differently after you deliver your message?

Step 2: List the hurdles. What audience interests and concerns do you need to address to get what you want?

Step 3: Lower the hurdles. Create the main elements of your message by persuasively addressing every audience interest and concern.

Step 4: Compose your message. Group the elements into categories of similar interests or concerns. Keep your message interesting and memorable by finding its natural story.

Step 5: Refine your message. Keep it simple. Deliver your message clearly with minimum detail and words needed to get your point across.

Connecting the Dots: The Interpersonal Presence Model

Back Stage: Where our thoughts, beliefs, values, feelings, attitudes, and biases reside. This is our internal life and who we believe ourselves to be. We are the only ones with direct access to it.

On Stage: Where we act with others. This is how we project ourselves through our eyes, faces, bodies, voices, the pace of our speech, and the architecture of our messages. It is what others use to create us in their minds. We have no direct access to it since we cannot see ourselves acting as others see us.

Our Audiences: Using the behavioral signals we send on stage, our audiences evaluate our behavior and come to conclusions about us. These impressions are always biased due to filtering of the present encounter based on past experience.

■

CHAPTER SEVEN

The Importance of Grooming and Dress

■

Our grooming and dress are typically the first things people notice about us, and they are important because of the messages they send. Are we seen as thoughtful, responsible, and sophisticated, or slightly unkempt, messy, and a little immature? Do we look like leaders or back office support? Our grooming and dress always send some kind of message, since there is no such thing as a neutral look. What follows are some simple rules for managing these messages.

Since gender differences affect the rules for business dress, we will discuss rules for men and women separately. There are, however, some fundamental rules for grooming and business dress that are not gender-specific.

Grooming

Good grooming starts with basic personal hygiene with a focus on teeth, breath, skin, and scent.

In addition to regularly brushing and flossing your teeth, pay attention to their color. Yellowing teeth stand out, usually causing their owners to smile less often and less naturally. If your teeth are yellow or stained, have them whitened or whiten them yourself. If they are noticeably crooked, consider orthodontia. Orthodontics has come a long way in recent years and now offers more than one option for straightening teeth. Oftentimes wire braces can be avoided. An investment in straight teeth is money well spent.

Make sure your breath is fresh. If you have a problem with bad breath, find out why and take appropriate action. Although breath mints won't do much for serious breath odor problems, they will freshen up your breath during the day, especially if you drink coffee.

Don't forget to take care of your skin. Healthy skin gives you a more vital and attractive appearance. To understand how this matters we only need look back to the very first televised presidential debate between Richard Nixon and Jack Kennedy. Nixon showed up for the debate recovering from a cold, looking pale and sallow with a pronounced (and somewhat sinister) five o'clock shadow. Kennedy was rested, bright eyed and slightly tanned, having been in California preparing for the debate and taking good care of himself for three days prior. Those who saw the debate on television gave it to Kennedy in a landslide, while those who listened on the radio were split almost evenly over who had won.

Finally, if you use aftershave, cologne, or perfume, use only a high quality product and use it sparingly. This is not the way you want to announce your arrival. Too much fragrance is a sure way to annoy others and it can be a problem for those who have allergic reactions to scents.

The Building Blocks of Dress

There are six building blocks of dress that create the foundation for the gender-specific discussions that follow. These are fashion, fit, fabric, color, quality, and coordination.

Fashion

There's an old saying that fashion is fickle, that it changes unexpectedly in unexpected ways for who knows what reasons. Nowhere is this more true than in how we dress. Hem lines go up and down, ties change in pattern and width, vests come and go, suits and jackets are oversized then sculpted, structured then relaxed, and the popularity of today's color palette is always giving way to tomorrow's. How do we navigate these changes with our business dress? Thoughtfully.

With a few exceptions for fashion-forward industries like advertising, design, and the fashion industry itself, business dress tends to be conservative, incorporating fashion changes over time and generally rejecting trendiness. This does not mean our business dress should be drab and lifeless: conservative does not mean dull. It can be both interesting and a unique personal expression. But be thoughtful about the look you want to achieve. Here are some things to think about that will help you dress well and appropriately for your work environment:

- **Pay attention to the general standards of dress in your business or profession.** Bankers and lawyers, for example, dress more formally than people in most other businesses. They usually wear suits, with men wearing ties. Other businesses have moved away from this, so think about the standard you will measure yourself against.
- **What kind of work environment are you in every day?** Is it professional services or manufacturing? Are you on the shop floor, working alone in an office, or spending time with clients?

Your dress should be appropriate to the environment you work in every day, with an eye to balancing comfort, utility, and style.

- **Dress better than you have to.** Don't limit your dress to meeting the minimum requirements. Go beyond the minimum and take pride in how you look. Just because you can get away with a cotton skirt, slacks, or jeans doesn't mean you should. A wool or wool blend could add a nice upscale touch. The same is true for shirts, blouses, and tops of all kinds. Layering can also add interest and spark to your look. Try a mock turtleneck under a shirt, or a light jersey or sleeveless sweater over one. You'll be surprised at the improvement. Spend a little time with the look you want to cultivate. Look at some upscale fashion magazines, catalogues, or websites; visit some local stores that are a notch up from your customary outlets; hire an image consultant or just find a helpful clerk at a respectable clothing or department store. It's well worth the effort.

- **Dress to the next level.** Don't limit yourself to dressing like your peers. If you want to advance in your organization, look to the next level. This is an excellent source of guidance for successful dress. At many large consulting companies, for example, partners, principals, and directors make a practice of wearing jackets, nice shirts, tops, or blouses, and wool slacks or skirts. Smart senior managers who aspire to move up copy what they see at the top.

- **How do the leaders in your company groom and dress, and how do they compare with your company's competition?** You may see some good examples of executive dress in your company by observing company leadership, but this isn't always the case. As we all know, some business leaders are not exemplary dressers, so take care following their lead. This is where observing competitive business leaders can help. If that's not possible or practical, you can observe how business leaders in general dress. Whether in person or through television, magazines, or other media, the important thing is to make yourself aware of what good executive dress looks like and find examples for guidance.

A note on business casual: You've probably noticed that we have not discussed "business casual" dress. That's because the term doesn't mean much beyond wearing clothes to work without a tie. Although some writers have tried to define business casual, like Sherry Maysonave in her book *Casual Power* (which I encourage you to read), business casual remains an elusive concept for most people. In part, this is because appropriate business dress is affected by all of the things we've just discussed, and in part because a lot of us are not very imaginative when it comes to how we look. So instead of trying to deal with the business casual concept, let's stay focused on the more objective things we can do to create an appropriate business look.

Fit

Clothing for business dress should have a relaxed, comfortable fit— neither too tight nor too loose. As a rule, if there is very little room between your skin and clothes, the fit is too tight. One sign of a too-tight fit is severe wrinkling after sitting, especially across the hips and in the legs. Clothes that are too large, on the other hand, look baggy and unkempt. They signal that you are either unaware of how you look or don't care much about it.

To avoid some problems of fit when buying clothes, be conscious of how *you* look in them, since you'll be the one wearing them. Many of us make the mistake of buying clothes because we like the style and love how the clothes look on a mannequin. We imagine that's how the clothes will look on us (though we probably know we're kidding ourselves). Don't fall into that trap. Most of us have some decidedly un-mannequin-like proportions that make the clothes fit in un-mannequin-like ways. Alterations can help, but only if the garment you are considering is a good basic fit for your body shape. If not, no amount of altering will do the job, nor will buying a size larger or smaller.

If you insist on buying a garment that doesn't fit, one of two things will happen. You won't wear it once you get it home, which will quickly erode your motivation for spending more time and money on dress, or you will look and feel less than your best in it. Instead, make an honest assessment of how the garment fits you and seek a second opinion—one that's not intended to push you into buying something you shouldn't buy. If the fit is good, go ahead and buy it, but if major surgery is required you're probably making a mistake. Clothes that fit well can do wonders for your appearance, helping to mask those flaws that you don't want to advertise, while poorly fitting clothes do just the opposite.

But what if you have a body shape or proportions not suited to off-the-rack clothing? Maybe you have long arms or legs, or short ones, broad shoulders relative to your waist, or vice versa, or some other proportion that is out of the ordinary. If that's the case you may want to consider made-to-measure clothing. Although typically more expensive than off-the-rack, made-to-measure can provide a fit for anyone whose proportions are significantly different from the general population.

Fabric

Fabric also plays an important role in fit. Differences in fabric type (wool, cotton, silk, etc.), weight, and weave, taken together, produce what is called drape, which refers to the way a garment hangs on your body. Drape is important because it affects the way the garment looks on you. A garment with good drape will always enhance your appearance, smoothing the little bumps and sags that lesser fabrics won't conceal.

You'll get the best drape from medium weight worsted, gabardine, or hard finish (very tight weave) wools. Wool can also be blended with other fabrics, such as silk or cotton, to enhance sheen and overall appearance. This, combined with the comfort and versatility of wool and wool blends, is the reason these are the fabrics of choice for upscale business dress. In warmer climates, hard finished tropical weight wool is a great fabric for jackets, slacks, and skirts. Although tropical weight wool has slightly less drape, well-made garments of high quality fabric will still flatter your physique.

Silk and silk blends are excellent choices for blouses, tops, and some shirts. Since the weight and weave of silk vary, as with wool, you can match it to the climate. Cotton is the fabric of choice for men's shirts, especially when wearing a tie. It can be dry cleaned, which causes some weaves to behave more like wools or silks, or laundered and lightly starched, which replaces the drape with a crisp, fresh look. Cotton offers an almost infinite variety of colors and patterns to choose from, so you can complement any outfit.

Color

It is difficult to overestimate the importance of color. By itself, color can noticeably enhance or detract from your appearance. Colors that are right for you will make you look healthy and energetic, even when you're not, while colors that are wrong will diminish your vitality and energy, in spite of how good you feel. So how do you know *your* colors? Fortunately, there's an entire industry waiting to help you with that challenge.

The foundation for identifying your best colors are the four color palettes that were created to match skin tone, hair, and eye color with the colors you should wear. The four color palettes are commonly referred to as Winter, Summer, Spring, and Fall (Autumn). If, for example, you have olive-toned skin, black hair, and hazel eyes, you are a winter. Your suggested suit or jacket colors are black, charcoal, navy, grey, grey-beige, and taupe. Your formal shirt colors are bright white and blue, or less formally, solids and combinations of stripes and muted plaids made of the dominant colors in the winter palette, such as intense hues of green, blue, burgundy, red, blue-red, purple, and fuchsia. Colors to avoid are olive, gold, rust, camel, yellow-green, and orange, especially if anywhere near your face.

The logic underlying this color palette scheme is the grouping of colors according to those with underlying cool (blue) tones, comprising Winter and Summer, and those with underlying warm (yellow) tones, Spring and Fall. These two groupings then serve as the basis for further defining the four palettes matched to skin, hair, and eyes. To determine which color palette (or combination of palettes) is best for you, consult one of the many books on color, or better yet, have your colors done by a professional color analyst. The table below can help you get started. If you span seasons your best colors will likely be the cooler ones.

Skin	Hair	Eyes	Color Palette
White, Dark Brown Black, Olive	Black, Brown, Silver Grey, Salt and Pepper, White Blonde, Silver Grey	Brown, Hazel, Blue, Grey-Blue, Grey-Green	**Winter:** Navy, Black, Charcoal Grey, Grey, Burgundy, Red, White, Chocolate Brown, Deep Blue, Purple
Pale Beige, Pink, Rosy, Grey Brown	Ash Blonde, Platinum Blonde, Brown, White,	Blue, Grey-Blue, Grey-Green, Grey, Hazel, Light Brown	**Summer:** Navy, Plum, Lavender, Slate Grey, Taupe, Rose Pink, Mauve, Rose Brown Pale Green, Raspberry
Golden, Ivory, Peach, Rosy, Brown	Golden Blonde, Strawberry Blonde, Auburn, Golden Brown, Golden Grey	Blue, Aqua, Green, Teal	**Spring:** Camel, Golden Brown, Peach, Ivory, Bright Green, Cream, Soft Blues, Periwinkle, Coral, Soft Yellow, Jade
Ivory, Peach, Copper, Golden Brown	Red, Copper, Chestnut, Auburn, Golden Grey	Dark Brown, Golden Brown, Amber, Hazel, Pale Green, Aqua	**Fall:** Turquoise, Orange, Gold, Emerald, Dark Brown, Mustard, Sea Blue, Royal Blue, Cream, Teal, Camel, Olive, Butterscotch, Ivory, Salmon

Quality

The rule on quality in clothing is to buy as much of it as you can afford. High quality garments fit better, look better, and last longer. Cuts are fuller, seam construction is better, and there is much more attention to detail. Although quality clothing usually costs more, if you take your time and shop sales at better stores, you can build an excellent wardrobe without spending a fortune.

When assessing the quality of a garment, look at the fabric. Is it natural or synthetic? Natural fibers will usually provide more quality than synthetics, although there are some good synthetics and excellent blends on the market today. Try the garment on and check the fit and drape (how the garment hangs on your body). You want it to have enough fabric weight and flexibility to compliment you by the way it hangs. Check the seams: are they tightly stitched and lying flat or poorly stitched and puckered? Have they been carefully finished or can you see loose threads? Examine both the exterior and interior. Are the trousers, slacks, or skirt lined? Higher quality garments are, ensuring greater comfort and reduced stress on fabric and seams. When you examine striped or patterned garments look for pattern matches at insertion points, such as the arms and pockets. Pattern matching is a big differentiator between higher and lower quality clothing. Compare shirts and blouses this way too, checking to make sure buttons are inset enough to allow an inch or so of overlap when the shirt or blouse is buttoned. Once you have compared some higher and lower quality clothing with these things in mind, you will be able to immediately spot the difference between the two.

To get the most out of the quality you buy, be sure to take proper care of your clothes. They will look better and last longer. Begin by hanging your clothes after wearing them. Don't just fold them over the back of a chair or drop them in a pile. For jackets, use a coat hanger with wide enough bars to support the shoulders. Look for a hanger with a soft hanger bar for slacks to avoid creasing across the legs. Loosely woven soft silk blouses, shirts, and tops should be stored folded so that their weight won't stretch the fabric. Harder finished silks and silk blends can be hung, but use a wooden hanger or a padded wire hanger. Laundered shirts can be hung on wire hangers. And give your clothes room to breathe in your closet by making sure they are not tightly packed against one another.

When having your clothes cleaned, use dry cleaning for wool and most silk garments, but always check the cleaning instructions on the garment label or tag. Also make sure your clothes are carefully pressed. Poorly pressed or wrinkled clothes send the wrong message, as do clothes that need mending. Shoes should always be polished and in good repair. Scuffed or worn shoes signal a lack of attention to the details of your appearance and send the wrong message. If the soles or heals of your shoes show wear, have them replaced. Give the same attention to briefcases, handbags, belts, scarves, jewelry, and other accessories.

Coordination

Business clothes are bought as suits or separates. With suits, which are at the formal end of business dress, much of the coordination is done for you, since the jacket and slacks, or skirt, are cut from the same cloth. You need only concern yourself with buying shirts, blouses, tops, ties, shoes, and accessories that complement the suit.

Less formal clothing, on the other hand, is bought piecemeal and it is up to you to make sure it is coordinated. Because of this, buying less formal dress is best done with a plan. One plan that works well is called capsule dressing. In capsule dressing, jackets become the coordinating garments in your wardrobe. Everything else you buy should go with one or more of them. Don't buy slacks, for instance, simply because you like them. Buy them because you like them and because you can wear them with one or more of your jackets.

Capsule dressing also provides a pecking order when matching your clothes. The jacket comes first, then coordinating slacks and/ or skirts. Then look for shirts, blouses, tops, and finally accessories such as belts, scarves, jewelry, and shoes. If you do this well, you will be able to mix *and* match your clothes, using a small number of jackets on a regular basis and getting the best return on your clothing investment.

Health and Fitness

The best investment you can make in yourself is your health and fitness. Eating right, staying hydrated, not drinking too much, getting enough sleep, and exercising can't be beat for giving you the real energy and energetic appearance you need to be the best you can be. Although attention to health and fitness requires setting aside personal time for physical exercise, as well as exercising some discipline with your diet, your returns can be enormous. Studies of people who work at keeping fit and healthy indicate that they have more energy at work, better concentration, are better prepared to handle adversity, and feel better throughout the day.

If you don't have a regular exercise program, start one. The ideal routine combines strength training and aerobics of some sort, be it walking, running, swimming, bicycling, elliptical, or a combination of them all. Find the exercises you enjoy and you will be much more likely to stick with a routine. Many people also find that a health club or gym offers the advantage of exercising with others, either informally or in structured classes that offer yoga, spinning, and aerobics of various skill levels and intensity.

In addition to exercising, give yourself a little private time every day. Use it to think and slow the world down. If you are overweight, lose the extra weight. You will look better, your clothes will fit better, and you'll feel better about yourself.

If you need a guiding principle for all of this, think in terms of moderation. Don't go on crash diets, fad diets, or crash exercise programs. You can't undo years of inattention to health and fitness overnight. Take your time, build slowly, and you will come to find these activities renewing and enjoyable.

Now let's turn our attention to gender-specific issues in grooming and dress.

Men

Hair and Nails

Always keep your hair neat, clean, and healthy. Hairstyles are generally best when shorter, especially as you age. Shorter styles create a more youthful appearance and are easy to maintain. If you choose to wear your hair longer, make sure you invest the time to keep it neat and styled. If you are balding, do not use a comb-over or toupee. Neither will effectively conceal hair loss, both are readily identifiable, and comb-overs are a real problem in all but the calmest conditions. Either create a style with the hair you have that satisfies you or add hair with a transplant.

Hair color for men is another area for caution. If you are considering coloring your hair, first seek the advice of a professional. Black hair, for example, will not color well if you want to keep it black. If you decide to go ahead with coloring, have it done professionally and maintain it diligently.

Facial hair in business is not the norm but is acceptable. However, the more of it you have the closer you get to the margin of acceptability. Full beards are the toughest to get away with, so if you wear one keep it very short and always freshly trimmed. Goatees and mustaches are a little more common but still need to be kept short and neat.

Remember too that the acceptability of facial hair is influenced by the culture of your company, so be aware of the impression it will make on others where you work.

Ear and nose hair should never be seen. To remove it, buy a trimmer and use it regularly. Whenever you shave, check to see if your nose and ear hair need trimming. Alternatively, ear hair can be permanently removed through an inexpensive and quick laser process offered by many dermatologists. Keep your eyebrows neatly trimmed, especially if they tend to be bushy. If your eyebrows are especially wide and/or close to joining together in the center of your forehead, you can have some of this hair removed with hot waxing, a service commonly offered by manicurists. This will make you look more energetic and accessible.

Hands are prominent features that others notice. Keep your nails clean and short with healthy cuticles, whether you do it yourself or use a manicurist. Hands that are not sparkling clean with well-groomed nails and healthy cuticles detract from a professional image.

Creating a Business Wardrobe

A basic executive business wardrobe for men includes both traditional business dress (business formal) and more casual attire. The foundation for business formal dress is a suit, while the foundation for more casual dress is a combination of sports jackets, blazers, and slacks (separates).

Traditional Business Dress (Business Formal): Depending on how often you will wear a suit, you may want only one or two. Suits that are excellent for anchoring your business formal wardrobe are single breasted, two- or three-button, in dark colors. The best colors are navy blue and charcoal grey, provided these work with your color palette, in either solid colors or with light chalk stripes.[16] These are powerful suits that will serve you well whatever the business formal occasion. If you buy more than one, you might want to get one in a two-button and another in a three-button style, since the looks are different.

The choice of pleated or plain front trousers is up to you, based on the way you look and feel in them. However, off-the-rack suits come with either one or the other, so a preference for one will limit your suit choices. This does not mean, however, that you should settle for pleated or plain front trousers simply because the suit you like happens to have them. Whatever your preferred look, you will eventually find a suit that satisfies all your requirements. Be patient and take your time: a suit is the single most expensive wardrobe investment you will make and one that should have lasting value. Get it right so you will look forward to wearing it and reap the return on your investment.

Once you've selected a suit, decide on cuffs or plain bottoms for the trousers. If the trousers are pleated, they should be cuffed with a slight or medium break in front. If you are tall, either break will work. If you are short or on the heavy side, go with a slight break. For plain front trousers the choice of cuffed or plain bottoms is up to you, but fashion changes often suggest one or the other. If you prefer braces (suspenders), make sure the trousers have buttons for them. If they don't, have the buttons sewn in when the pants are being altered. Braces are best worn with cuffed trousers, except for tuxedo trousers, which are never cuffed.

Business dress shirts should be long sleeve and made of high quality cotton in broadcloth, pinpoint oxford, or end-on-end weave. Make sure you have at least one or two in solid white and blue, again making allowances for your individual color palette, with either straight or tab collars. A contrasting white collar is a nice dressy

---

16 Navy blue and charcoal grey are the traditional power colors. However, if they are wrong for your color palette, browns can also work. Presidents Ronald Reagan and Bill Clinton demonstrated this.

touch for blue shirts, and both the white and blue shirts could be a mix of conventional or barrel sleeves, with one- or two-button cuffs, or French cuffs.

Since these are shirts you will wear with your suits, select them with your suits in mind. Better yet, have the suit with you when you buy the shirts if you are buying anything other than bright white.

Casual Dress: When choosing separates, remember capsule dressing guidelines: coordinate slacks, shirts, and accessories with the jacket. Two versatile jackets to have in your wardrobe are a solid black and a solid blue blazer. Both blazers coordinate well with all shades of grey slacks plus taupe and tan. As you mix the grey and tan slacks with either the black or blue jacket, you will create a totally new look. You might also consider a muted pattern in the slacks since there is nothing in either jacket to conflict with it. Both the jackets and slacks should be wool or a wool blend. Avoid cotton chinos and khakis in your casual business wardrobe. This is a look best saved for weekends.

An excellent choice of material for either jacket is wool crepe. It has great drape, is a little less structured than harder finished wool, and is very comfortable to wear. A wool crepe jacket also looks great with patch pockets, which provide more flexibility in dressing it up or down. If you spend most of your time in a warmer climate, think about tropical wools and wool worsted fabrics for the slacks. If you are frequently in colder weather, you can buy heavier weights and make seasonal adjustments.

If you decide to buy seasonal clothing, solid color cashmere and wool blended jackets are terrific for colder months. They are easy to find in navy, black, grey, and camel, and are very versatile. Just remember what colors you wear well when buying these jackets, and if you decide to jump out of your color season, make sure you have one of your best colors framing your face.

Muted plaids, subtle patterns, and houndstooth jackets are another option for casual dress. Although more challenging when matching slacks and shirts, they add variety to your wardrobe. You can coordinate slacks with the dominant jacket color or pick up one of the colors in the pattern.

Your casual shirts should be mostly long sleeve, high quality cotton, but can have greater variety in collar styles, pattern, and color than business formal. Traditional button-down, hidden button-down (sometimes called European button-down), and several variations of the straight collar are readily available. When selected carefully, stripes, dressy checks, and subtle patterns can add interest to your wardrobe and give it a nice change of pace. But don't go overboard. Stick with more subtle patterns and with stripes or checks that work with or without a tie.

In addition to your cotton shirts, buy some long sleeve silks in your best solid colors. They are a nice way to add variety to your business dress. Long sleeve knit pullovers in blended silk with collars or mock turtlenecks can also add variety and interest, plus they look great with jackets and blazers. If you decide to wear polo shirts for your most casual days, make sure they are a high quality silk blend or mercerized cotton, and think about wearing an unstructured sport jacket with them. You aren't on the golf course at work, even on your most casual days, so don't look like it. Other than the occasional polo shirt, you should not wear short sleeve shirts to work.

Always wear an undershirt of some kind with your cotton shirts, but make sure it never shows. V-neck or tank top styles will ensure that you are never caught with your white crew-neck undershirt peeking out of the triangle directly under your chin. If you wear any color undershirt other than white, make sure the color doesn't show through; this holds true for any undergarment.

Just because you don't have to wear a tie to work doesn't mean you shouldn't. Try wearing one once in a while with the idea of making your casual dress more interesting and uniquely you. Go for a dressy informal look by combining an interesting stripe or pattern dress shirt with a solid or woven fabric tie. You can get some ideas by looking through men's clothing catalogs for interesting and dressy casual shirt-and-tie combinations.

Customization: When buying casual shirts, whether you intend to wear them with a tie or without, consider customization. Today, several manufacturers offer fabric, collar, and cuff style options, as well as contrasting white collars, for the same price as higher-end, off-the-shelf shirts. Even such minimal customization (also called semi-custom) gives you greater choice in matching shirt color, pattern, and style to your jackets and slacks. Another plus with custom shirts is sizing. If your arms and neck are not standard proportions for off-the-shelf sport shirts, you will consistently have a problem with sleeves being too long or too short and/or the body of the shirt not fitting well. At a minimum, customization offers you the ability to pick your shirting material and specify both neck size and sleeve length. Semi-custom shirt options vary by manufacturer so see what's available. You can also buy made-to-measure shirts that are completely crafted for you. Better made-to-measure shirts are expensive but worth it if you are hard to fit or want something really special in your wardrobe.

Accessories: Accessories for men include belts, ties, braces (suspenders), shoes, socks, jewelry, glasses, and handkerchiefs. Since this is not a long list, make sure every accessory you select counts. It should stand out in both quality and style.

- **Belts:** High quality belts can be some of the most interesting accessories in a man's wardrobe. When selecting one, first be sure you are buying quality in both the leather and buckle hardware. There are three good reasons for this. First, high quality leather resists showing wear, especially on the front where the belt passes through the buckle, and it won't crack. Second, plating on high quality buckles and metal keeper loops will not discolor or wear off, exposing the underlying metal. Better plating also conceals scratches. Third, higher quality belts offer sophisticated styling and attention to detail, the things you want in an important accessory. When selecting a belt to wear with a suit, choose something that is simple and sophisticated, usually in black or brown. For a more casual look, think about the slacks, shirts, and jackets you will wear it with, since the choices available in hides or skins (cow, lizard, alligator, ostrich, etc.), combined with color, styling, and buckle hardware, can really add interest to your more casual business look.

- **Ties:** If belts are one of the most interesting accessories for men, ties are the most noticed. When selecting ties for your suits, stay with simple, muted patterns, tone-on-tone weaves, and regimental stripes, which are now staging a comeback. Make sure you buy high quality ties, which usually means high quality silk with good backing. A high quality tie is easier to tie into a good looking knot and will hold the knot better than a lower quality tie. Ties for a less formal look can be less conservative, but must still show good fashion sense, so make sure they are tasteful and match your outfits, whether or not they include a jacket or light cardigan sweater. Except for true formal dress, stay away from bow ties.

- **Braces (Suspenders):** Braces are a nice alternative to wearing a belt with a suit, especially if you are looking to add some sophistication. Although you have a variety of choices here, it's best to stay with something on the conservative side. Think about solid colors, with the pattern defined by the weave in the fabric, and subtle color patterns and stripes. Color selection should coordinate with the suit and shirt. Silk is the best fabric for braces, with leather extensions in the front and back for buttoning them to your trousers. Never wear clip-on suspenders or suspenders and a belt; both are fashion gaffes.

- **Shoes:** Wear shoes with laces or cross-strap buckles whenever you wear a suit with a tie. Suits are best finished with the more formal look these basic styles provide. Both styles look good in either cap or split toe. There are numerous slip-on and oxford shoe styles and color combinations available to complement the more casual wardrobe, so you can use your imagination here—but don't overdo it. High quality tassel or penny loafers with leather soles in black, brown, or cordovan are always excellent choices. Stay away from boat shoes and shoes with excessive design accents, such as single or double kiltie fringe fronts with tassels. This results in a cumbersome, cluttered look. The same is true when you mix leather shoe colors, so be careful here as well. Keep in mind that the simpler shoe is often the better, more stylish, choice.

- **Socks:** Always wear socks to work. Although it is fashionable these days to go without them, this should be saved for off-work time. Match your socks to either your shoes or slacks and be careful with socks that draw attention to your feet, such as argyles. Stay with colors and subtle patterns that smoothly transition from slacks to shoes. When you sit, never let skin show between the top of your sock and the bottom of your pant leg. You can prevent this by wearing over-calf socks or by simply being attentive to keeping mid-calf socks up. Arguments against over-calf socks are that they can be too warm and often cause static cling with lighter weight wools. From the standpoint of fashion, either works. Choose whatever you like best.

- **Jewelry:** When it comes to jewelry, keep it simple. A watch, no more than one ring on the third finger of each hand, and cuff links for French cuffs. If you wear a bracelet on your non-watch wrist, keep it high quality and conservative. They are typically not part of a business look, and are out of place with formal business attire. Keep rings and cuff links simple: gold or silver with the optional stone. If you wear two rings, wear a stone in only one of them, if at all.

- **Glasses:** Glasses allow you to make a fashion statement with the frames. Frame shape and color, however, should complement your coloring and the shape of your face. Make sure the lenses have a non-glare coating, which will allow others to see your eyes.
- **Handkerchiefs:** These are decorative handkerchiefs, also called pocket stuffers. Typically made of colorful silk in solids and patterns, they are also available in high quality white cotton. They add visual interest and integration to an outfit when folded or "stuffed" into the breast pocket of a suit or jacket. However, handkerchiefs should be reserved for times when you want a dressier, upscale, or more sophisticated look.

Women

Hair, Makeup, and Nails

Hair should always be clean, healthy, and neatly kept. Hairstyles for women in business are generally best when shorter, if for no other reason than shorter styles take less time to groom. Longer styles are certainly acceptable, but if you wear a longer style, make sure you take the time to manage it. Also be sure to keep your hair out of your face. Besides being distracting, when your hairstyle partially covers your face it diminishes your power and does not project a business image. It will also likely cause you to develop habitual head and hand movements to move the hair out of your face, which is distracting. If you are younger and trying to project a more powerful image, keeping your hair pulled back and out of your face is a must.

Professional hair coloring is now more the norm than the exception for businesswomen, but there are several things to keep in mind if you color your hair. First, be attentive to its condition. Never let it look brittle or bleached out. Take whatever steps you must to keep it looking healthy. Second, don't change colors overnight. Do it gradually and make sure the new color complements your complexion. Since your complexion will lighten as you age, keep the coloring lighter than your original hair color. Dying your hair black or something close to it, for example, will not work as you get older. The color will be too severe. Keeping it lighter will help soften wrinkles and will work better with your complexion. Finally, be sure to maintain the color; don't wait until your roots are showing to do a touch-up.

If your hair is graying and you decide not to color it, be attentive to how it works with the colors in your wardrobe. You may need to make some adjustments in the color palette you've been using.

If you have facial hair, you can have it removed with hot waxing or, more permanently, with laser treatments, which are available from many dermatologists. Also, keep your eyebrows plucked and trimmed and pay attention to the space between them. If you have heavy eyebrows that extend across your forehead, make sure you have some of the hair removed, especially where the eyebrows want to join together. Hot waxing and threading are excellent ways to do this and are available at most manicure salons. Finally, if you choose to curl your eyelashes and use mascara, don't overdo it. This is a case where too little is far better than too much!

Consider wearing makeup if you don't wear it now. Applied lightly and carefully, it almost always creates a healthier, more sophisticated look. The operative words, of course, are lightly and carefully. Be conservative. Apply your makeup in a well-lit environment, and pay attention to the blending. Err on the side of underdone, especially as you get older. Too much makeup is worse than none at all.

Keep your nails no longer than medium length and your cuticles healthy. Nails that are not well cared for detract from a professional image. When coloring your nails, your best bet is to stay conservative. If you want to project a solid business persona, avoid nail art and unusual colors, including black.

Creating a Business Wardrobe

A basic executive business wardrobe for women includes both traditional business dress (business formal) and casual business attire, the same as for men. The good news is that in today's business environment women are no longer expected to dress like men. This provides you with the flexibility to express yourself in your dress without having to worry about conforming to male styles and standards.

Traditional Business Dress (Business Formal): Unlike men, whose business formal dress comprises traditional business suits in a narrow spectrum of colors, women have many choices. Along with the usual tailored looks in grey and navy, a host of other cuts, styles, and colors are yours to choose from. A suit jacket, for example, can be cut to the waist or the hip and have either a tailored or more relaxed fit. It might go with a traditional knee-length skirt or be part of a pantsuit, now widely accepted as business formal.

When choosing any of these suits, stick with wool, wool blends, and some of the newer synthetics. Look for deeper colors that work well with your coloration in solids, tweeds, houndstooth, and plaids. Stay away from pastels, which convey neither power nor authority. The deeper colors in your color palette are much better options. Also consider suits that have contrasting jackets, with or without coordinating patterns. When carefully chosen they are nice additions to a basic wardrobe. If you choose a pantsuit, wear the shoes you will pair with it (or shoes with the same style and heel height) when having the pants hemmed. The pants are best left uncuffed with only a slight break in front. If you are on the heavier or shorter side, have the pants hemmed to the top of your shoe without a break.

As your business formal wardrobe expands, two-piece dresses and high quality knits are great alternatives to a suit. When accessorized in creative and interesting ways, they provide all the sophistication and formality of a suit but with a different look. Again, stay with the deeper, stronger colors that work with your complexion, hair, and eyes.

When selecting blouses and tops for your business suits, keep them simple. Stay away from frills and lace, which do not project a professional business image and will detract from your power and authority. When making your selections, start with the fabric. Always select fabrics that are compatible with the fabric of your suit. If you are buying for a silk blend or light polyester suit, for example, select blouses and tops that have the same fabric weight and appearance, avoiding cottons. If you want to wear cottons, save them for your heavier wool suits. Although you will typically want to select colors and simple color patterns that contrast nicely with your suit, you can also select colors with the same tonality of the suit, creating a tone-on-tone effect.

Collar styling is another consideration, with round, rounded square, V-neck, boat neck, tailored collar, and collarless styles all offering nice options. Make sure, however, that the style you select will not show cleavage, which is never acceptable at work. Finally, decide on sleeve length. Long sleeves, short sleeves, or three-quarter length sleeves all work well with a suit.

Casual Dress: When choosing separates, remember capsule dressing guidelines: Pants, skirts, blouses, tops, and accessories should all coordinate with one or more of your jackets. The jacket, which is the foundation for each of your casual ensembles, sets the pace for everything else. As with suits, there is a broad range of color, style, and fabric options in jackets, so go for versatility. Start with something basic that will give you the largest number of mix and match options.

One excellent choice is a black-and-white wool houndstooth, which illustrates the capsule dressing idea. Simple, straight skirts in black, white, and red, and pants in black-and-white will all work with it, as will tops in the same colors. This gives you the opportunity to mix and match skirts, pants, and tops of different colors with one jacket, creating a different look with each outfit. The wool houndstooth also allows you to wear cotton blouses with more tailored collar styles. If jeans are the norm for casual Fridays where you work, you can even wear designer jeans with the jacket, along with a tailored cotton blouse, creating a look that is upscale and casual at the same time. Thoughtful accessorizing creates even more looks using these same basic pieces.

This mixing and matching is also easily done with navy, black, grey, and camel blazers in single- and double-breasted styles, as well as many patterns and plaids. In addition to color, there is also enormous variety in style and fabric. Along with the blouses and tops mentioned so far, there are turtlenecks and mock turtlenecks that create a fashionable look when paired with almost any jacket and pant or skirt combination.

Accessories: Women's accessories consist of belts, scarves, shoes, hosiery, jewelry, and glasses. Used creatively, these are the things that can make an outfit really come to life. To get pop from your accessories, however, you must think about balance and blending. Balance means keeping your accessories from overpowering your outfit and dominating your look instead of shaping and sharpening it. A balanced look is a finished look where your accessories add neither too much nor too little. Too much accessorizing creates a heavy, overdone look, with too much going on. Too little accessorizing leaves you looking unfinished.

Blending is the partner of balance. Seek a coordinating theme in your accessorizing, a theme that ties your accessories and outfit together to form an integrated whole. At a minimum, blending involves coordinating color, style, and material. If, for example, you are wearing a grey silk or polyester top with a plain grey pearl necklace (with no visible metal setting), you will have a challenge making yellow gold earrings work. The hard finish of the metal will not integrate well with the softness of the pearls and the color of the yellow gold will look out of place. Poor blending makes one or more of your accessories stand out in unwanted ways, a sign your accessorizing lacks coordination. You can mix different textures, materials, colors, and styles, but always do so with a coordinating theme in mind.

Belts: Women's belts come in just about every conceivable material, color, width, length, and buckle style, presenting myriad options for creative accessorizing. However, when selecting a belt to wear with a suit, stay on the conservative side. Choose a well-made leather belt in real or faux hide with a high quality buckle.

The color can either match the color of your suit or provide a contrast. For example, when wearing a black or grey suit, try a simple black belt in shiny alligator or flat ostrich. The buckle could be wrapped in the same hide as the belt or be made of silver or chrome.

Scarves: Like belts, scarves offer a range of choices in both color and pattern. When selecting one, go for a color that adds energy to your outfit or fits a coordinating theme. If, for example you want to add a third color to an outfit for a little extra punch, a scarf is a good solution. Dressed in a black straight skirt or slacks with a black top and red hip-length jacket, you will look even better with a red, white, and black scarf tied at the neck. With some outfits, a scarf can be the element that unites the ensemble. Taupe slacks and top, for example, with an unstructured blue blazer can be pulled together with a scarf containing blue and taupe. A scarf can also add interest through the way you tie it, especially if you are going for a monochromatic look. Some options include elongated, similar to a man's necktie; triangular, worn across the back of the shoulders with the knot in front (similar to the way sweaters are sometimes worn); and a wrap high around the neck, with the points from the knot worn at the front or side. The only warning here is not to let the color or the pattern be too much of a distraction. A scarf can add a lot, but it should make sense with the rest of your outfit.

Shoes: A mid-heel pump (1½- to 2½-inch heels) is an excellent shoe choice and one that will never be wrong. Although you should stay on the conservative side, very pointed styles are now popular and appropriate for business dress. Be conservative with shoe color, matching it to your belt or outfit. Matching to your outfit works well when you are going for a monochromatic look. Avoid white completely, substituting beige or taupe. For work styles, stay away from sandals, mules, and any shoe with an open toe. Although some people think open-toe shoes are acceptable for business wear, they are not. Save them for leisure activities. Also think about comfort when buying shoes. Don't let style push you to buy uncomfortable shoes. With patience, you can find a shoe that satisfies both your style and comfort requirements. Finally, look for quality in your shoes. Higher quality shoes will be more comfortable, look better, and last longer.

Hosiery: Match your stockings to your shoes, dresses, skirts, and pants. Your best bets are ultra-sheer shades, a much better look for business dress than textures or opaque. Ultra-sheer shades matched to your outfit create a smooth visual line from foot to waist, enhancing your stature. They can also do a lot to bring out the recessive colors in your ensemble, but be careful of colors that contrast with your outfit. They create a visual break that will make you look shorter and your legs larger. Avoid white stockings completely, substituting skin tones.

Jewelry: Jewelry options include earrings, necklaces, watches, bracelets, rings, and broaches. Earrings are a must to give you a finished look. They frame your face and provide additional color and visual interest. Select earrings in gold, white gold, silver, pearl, and darker or more vivid stone colors, such as blue, black, and black and gold. When buying earrings, be aware that they should not match the shape of your face. For example, if you have a round face, look for elongated shapes in rectangles and ovals. If you have an oblong face, try round or triangular shapes. If you choose a hoop earring, make sure it is simple and proportional to your size. Don't choose long dangling earrings that sway and distract. And stay away from multi-colored enamel and rhinestones, which are not part of an executive wardrobe.

Necklaces must coordinate with your earrings. Generally, pearls go with pearls and metal goes with metal and metal-stone combinations. If your earrings have a burnished finish, so should your necklace, and vice versa. If you wear a watch, wear the best you can afford. It's good to have one watch in silver tones and another in gold, but if you can only afford one, go with the jewelry color you most often wear. Be careful with bracelets. If you wear one, make sure it coordinates with your other jewelry and doesn't have multiple bands that jangle. Limit the number of rings you wear as well. Although women can wear multiple rings, don't get carried away.

Glasses: Glasses can make a fashion statement with the color, shape, and weight of the frames. Frame shape and color, however, should complement your coloring and the shape of your face. Make sure the lenses of your glasses have a non-glare coating so that people can see your eyes.

The Importance of Grooming and Dress

The Six Building Blocks of Dress

1. Fashion

- Pay attention to the general standards of dress in your business or profession.
- Dress appropriate to the environment you work in.
- Dress better than you have to.
- Dress to the next level.
- Pay attention to how the leaders in your business dress and how they compare with your company's competition.

2. Fit

- Relaxed and comfortable—neither too tight nor too loose.
- Be conscious of how the clothes you are considering look on you, not on the mannequin.
- If major alterations are required, keep looking.
- Made-to-measure clothing is an option, especially for shapes and sizes that are significantly different from the general population.

3. Fabric

- Look for good drape when you shop; it will enhance your appearance.
- Buy natural fibers, especially wool, cotton, and silk blends.

4. Color

- It is difficult to overestimate the importance of color. By itself, color can noticeably enhance or detract from your appearance.
- Use the color palettes on page 100 as the basis for identifying your best colors.

5. Quality

- Buy as much quality as you can afford. High quality garments fit better, look better, and last longer.
- Examine the fabric (natural or synthetic), the fit and drape, the seams (should lay flat), the finish, and the way patterns match at insertion points.
- Take care of your clothes after wearing them with proper hangers and breathing room in your closet.

6. Coordination

- Use the principles of capsule dressing to make coordinating your wardrobe easy and efficient: jackets are the coordinating garment, then slacks

■

CHAPTER EIGHT

Creating and Delivering Executive Messages

■

Good executive messages have three things in common: unambiguous purpose, tight crafting, and crisp delivery. Because of this they are uncommonly clear and easy to understand. They are called executive messages because they are characteristic of the way our most powerful and influential leaders communicate.

One important characteristic of a tightly crafted, crisply delivered executive message is the economical use of detail. It never clutters the message and is used solely to support the conclusions and points being made. Detail is never used to embellish a theme, provide information that is simply nice to have from the speaker's point of view, or impress the audience with the speaker's knowledge of the subject.

The best executive messages also have an internal logic that follows a story format, tightly connecting one point to the next with a good narrative flow. We don't get lost when we listen to good executive messages. Even when we don't agree with what's being said, we are never confused by it. Their clarity and focus provide unambiguous direction and clear choices for decision-making.

Creating Executive Messages

While there are many ways to create a good executive message, almost all methods follow some kind of systematic process. I developed the Message Architecture™ method several years ago in response to persistent and widespread problems clients were having with clarity and wordiness, causing them to get to the point late and without a good story. Message Architecture™ addresses these issues with a five step, audience-centric framework that makes purpose, clarity, and narrative the centerpieces of message creation. It is also easy to use and applicable to all content and communication styles, so it is not surprising that Message Architecture™ is becoming the method of choice at companies large and small.

The first three steps of the Message Architecture™ method should be followed in order, as they guide you through identifying the key points that will become the content of your message. Once you have carefully worked through these steps you will be ready to compose the message you will deliver. If you did good homework in the first three steps, you will have the content you need to build a concise, convincing, and targeted message, one that draws your audience in and keeps their attention. The final step is simply to review, refine, and practice your message. There is no substitute for practicing your delivery out loud. This will help you develop cadence and flow in your spoken words, especially when transitioning from one thought to another, and point up any awkward or wordy spots that need refinement.

Message Architecture™

The five steps of the Message Architecture™ method are as straightforward as the messages they will help you develop. In this chapter we'll start with a quick review of the steps in their most concise form to help you appreciate their logical simplicity. Then we'll study each step in more detail, and finally review three examples that illustrate how the method works in practice.

1. **Say what you want:** write in one crystal clear statement what you want from your message, then write down why you want it, and how you plan to get it.
2. **List the hurdles:** make a list of the interests, concerns, and objections your audience will have that could prevent you from getting what you want.
3. **Lower the hurdles:** compose your most persuasive arguments to address each interest, concern, and objection
4. **Compose your message:** assemble your message by logically tying your arguments together in a compelling and memorable narrative.
5. **Refine your message:** keep it is simple, easy to follow, and easy to understand.

Step 1: Say what you want
Write the *what* (and *why*, and *how*) of your message

Until you know *exactly* what you want your audience to think or do differently as a result of hearing your message, you will not be able to clearly articulate that message.

It is important to capture what you want from your message in a single, concise statement using measurable terms—a *want* statement, if you will. For example, it is not enough to say "I would like the support of the senior leadership team." This is too general and will not help you identify why you might not get the support you want. The statement must include specifics on how the senior leadership team will show their support. It is this specificity that really drives clarity, as you will see when analyzing the three examples presented below. Until you can be specific enough to identify what you want in a clearly written statement with measurable outcomes, you will not be ready for the next Message Architecture™ step.

It is also important to clearly articulate *why* you want what you want. What you want is almost always in service of something else, some end game. You might, for example, want approval to spend money that will produce a return. Here the potential return is the end game. It is the vision—the *why*.

The *how* of message creation is about implementation and is the way you are going to do something. In the previous paragraph, for example, it is *how* you are going to spend the money you are asking for to produce the return. When developing executive messages it is critical that the *how* be focused, clear, and specific, as the details of execution often generate the most pushback.

Step 2: List the hurdles
Identify audience interests, concerns, and objections

Having identified what you want from your message, you can begin to think more clearly about the fears, concerns, interests, and questions—the hurdles—that might stand in the way of getting it. Investigate all potential objections and what your audience needs to know that will help them give you what you want. What are their main concerns and sticking points? What are they interested in or afraid of? If you cannot identify and address these questions completely, you will be guessing at what you need to talk about and it is unlikely you will create a message that is either direct or compelling. Take the time now and make the effort to know with certainty the issues and concerns of your audience.

Sometimes these issues are obvious and sometimes they are not. Often some digging is needed to identify all of them. This is time well spent, as getting what you want will depend on comprehensively completing this step. The results will define what you address. As you identify these issues and obstacles, don't be concerned with the elegance of your writing or even complete sentences. You are simply *capturing* them. Feel free to record this information rather than writing it. Just be sure that you are writing or speaking from the point of view of your audience.

It is critical to remember that if you miss something important here you will not be prepared to address it when it comes up while you are delivering your message, as it surely will. This will not only derail your argument, it will make you look like you don't understand what is important, or like you are simply unprepared. Missing a *single* point in this way can diminish your credibility.

Finally, comprehensively completing this step helps you think better on your feet. Considering a topic from your audience's point of view is a powerful tool as it gives you the ability to quickly and empathetically respond to objections, demonstrating forethought as well as respect. This kind of preparation can also balance the need to demonstrate absolute expertise on any given point: it is the *effort* and desire to connect with your audience that will be most impactful in handling key audience objections and help to open doors to get what you want from your message.

Step 3: Lower the hurdles
Address each interest, concern, and objection

This is where you begin developing the content for your presentation. It starts simply, by taking the hurdles you identified in Step 2 and creating the most persuasive argument(s) to address, or lower, each of them. Never gloss over or try to finesse any of these points. If you fail to address all of them, your audience will think that you are not well informed, or that you are minimizing or ignoring a concern because you don't have an answer for it—or both. Either will become a new hurdle to getting what you want.

As you work through your arguments for each of the points you must address, think about them one at a time, asking the question, "What can I say to effectively deal with this issue or question?" Never rush this process. Play with ideas a little and see what happens. The results can be surprising. Sometimes a very persuasive argument is right in front of you, unnoticed. At other times you may find you're trying to do too much with a single message and need to insert more steps in the path to getting what you ultimately want.

Step 4: Compose your message
Assemble your arguments in a compelling and memorable narrative

The best messages have a narrative or story quality. This results from the message elements flowing in a way that both enhances the story and builds narrative tension that pulls the audience in and forward.

It is up to you find that narrative and put your message together in a way that gets the points across as powerfully as possible. This involves tightly coupling the persuasive arguments from Step 3 with the audience concerns from Step 2 in a seamless delivery that clearly associates the *tension* of each objection with the *resolution* of your solution. Never make your audience work to get the story. A compelling narrative will accomplish three things: it will add significant persuasiveness to your message, it will make your message easier to remember, and it will make your story easier to tell.

But to create a compelling narrative you must first be able to clearly and respectfully articulate the concerns, fears, and issues of your audience without looking down on them or brushing them aside. As you begin to do this, group them by similarity. Although it may at first seem like you have many elements to deal with, they will typically fit into a small number of groups. This grouping will help you create a story that flows, as you will see in the examples that follow. With this mindset you can create a story that is built on clearly stated concerns (hurdles), agreement with others that these concerns should be addressed (common purpose), thoughtful questions or observations about how those concerns might be met (tension), and proposed solutions to those concerns (resolution, lowered hurdles). Using empathy to build a concern-centered narrative will bring the power of good storytelling to your message.

On a practical note, it is very important to get all of this out of your head by practicing *out loud*. Reading a book to yourself and telling that same story to someone involve different parts of your brain, and executive messages are no different. Speaking your message will allow you to practice transitions, pauses, inflection, eye contact—all important aspects of good message delivery that are not a part of the process of constructing the message. As you practice speaking your message you may even run across wording that sounded okay on the page or in your head, but doesn't work when spoken out loud. Practicing out loud gives you an opportunity to revise and optimize your message so that it sounds natural and persuasive when spoken. Speaking your message, especially if you can find a willing test audience, will also provide a measure of "muscle memory," an extremely helpful outcome of practice that can sometimes save the day when your head may forget a point that, having spoken it a few times, your mouth may nonetheless remember. Seasoned speakers will attest to this. But remember, practice is for testing and familiarity, *not* for memorization. Do not try to polish it to perfection and then robotically repeat it that way every time. This will drain the energy out of your message and make it sound canned and mechanical. Use practice (and a good dose of it) to check the organization and flow of your narrative and to ensure graceful transitions when going from one idea to the next.

Step 5: Refine your message
Keep it is simple, easy to follow, and easy to understand

Finally, and simply, keep it simple. Always let your audience know why they are there and what you want from them. Never make them guess at what you want or how they fit into the picture. Are you looking for money, agreement on a course of action, their time, their approval, resources, or something else? Whatever it is, they need to know quickly and specifically.

A very effective way to refine and simplify your message is to start it, *in the first statements after your greeting*, with the *what*, *why*, and *how* from Step 1, often leading with the *why* to clearly establish the context or vision for what you want from them. As in the examples that follow, these statements should be crystal clear and direct, with no unnecessary words clouding the issue. You should be able to do this in two or three concise sentences. When you encounter difficulty constructing these statements, it is likely that what you want and the role your audience will play in getting it are probably not as clear as you had thought. Take note that a failure with this opening statement will seriously weaken even the strongest message.

The goal of refining your message is to make it easy to understand. Never make your audience work to understand what you want or what you are saying. They won't. If you haven't done your homework, they will tune you out and move on to other things, whether they intend to or not.

As you deliver your message, keep it simple for the duration. Use direct language that will be easily understood by all members of your audience. Word-like sounds and fillers, such as *umm*, *ah*, *like*, and *you know*, are out. And remember, a little silence is golden. Always speak slowly and use pauses when changing direction, introducing new thoughts, or asking your audience to think about something.

Putting the Method to Work

Let's look at three examples that illustrate how the method works in practice. Each one deals with a different type of *want* from the speaker. They all involve getting audience approval—first for an alternative use of office space, then for a rezoning request, and finally for project financing. Although each employs the Message Architecture™ method in the same way, the resulting three messages—each delivered as a presentation—are quite different. Each example takes us through the first three steps in the process. As we will see, Message Architecture™ provides an overarching structure for any message, so it is compatible with almost any presentation methodology.

Example A: Proposing an alternative way to use office space

This presentation started out with the speaker wanting to get support for "hoteling," an office space concept that assigns offices to people on a temporary basis, usually daily or weekly. Hoteling is popular in consulting and other professions where office users spend most of their time away from their offices.

Step 1: Say what you want
Orienting Question: *What do I want my audience (of one or many) to think or do differently as a result of my message?*

The answer to this question was vague at first. The speaker said he simply wanted to get management to support his proposal. But how would he know when he had their support?

When answers are vague, there are two questions that can help: 1) from whom, specifically, do we want the support, and 2) what does that support look like? In this example, the support was to come from the speaker's managing partner and his executive team, and consisted of approval to move forward with his hoteling proposal.

To complete our work with this step, the answers to two follow-up questions will help clarify and shape—if not completely change—how we will move forward with message creation. The first question addresses *why* we want what we want, the second *how* we will achieve our objective.

So *why*, then, did our speaker want to move forward with his hoteling proposal? He wanted to save money by decreasing the amount of leased office space the firm would need. Facilities management was an important part of his job and he could realize considerable savings by leasing less space. Notice, however, that this was not the way he originally framed his message. Instead, he focused on the details of *how* he would get these savings, sacrificing message context and the bigger picture in the process. In effect, he put the cart before the horse.

When we do this, and we do it all too frequently, we jump too far ahead of our audience. We fail to provide them with the context for our message—*the big picture*—and force them to either figure it out for themselves or interrupt us with questions that derail or confuse our message. Answering the question of *why* we want what we want takes care of this problem by clearly defining the bigger picture, or the end game, up front.

Turning to *how* the speaker would save money for the firm leads us to what he said he wanted in the first place, which was a hoteling solution for decreasing leased office space. However, within the context of saving money for the firm through more efficient facility management, we can see that hoteling is only one of several possible solutions. This allows the *how* to be reframed more broadly as securing agreement on an alternative approach to using office space rather than a specific, prescriptive way to do it. This is no minor point. The audience will first need to agree to reducing office space (which may be a proposal in itself) and then will want to know if alternatives to hoteling have been explored. Why is hoteling the best option if this remains the speaker's preferred solution?

Failure to separate the *what, why*, and *how* in our messages is often responsible for much of the confusion our audiences experience. Unanticipated questions can also derail our delivery effort. In the end, the speaker in our example elected to go with the broader idea of proposing an alternative use of office space in the interest of saving the firm money, and he used hoteling as one of the proven ways to do it.

Step 2: List the hurdles

Orienting Question: *What are the most important interests, issues, questions, concerns, or fears of my audience that will prevent me from getting what I want?*

For the speaker in this example, answering this question comprehensively required some additional digging. He worked behind the scenes with his idea for hoteling, asking members of the executive committee how they felt about the way space was being used and gauging their interest in changing what they were currently doing. He also floated hoteling as an option, which gave him the opportunity to gauge the reaction of his audience and assess their concerns before his formal presentation. Here are some of the concerns he found:

- How are we using our office space today?
- How much of our space is vacant, and how much of the time?
- How much money can we save by taking a different approach?
- How would the new approach work?
- What are the pluses and minuses of a new approach?
- Who will be affected by the change and how is that decision being made?
- How much resistance are we likely to get from associates who will be affected by the change?
- What are the plans to get people on board with the change and ensure morale doesn't suffer?
- How do we proceed? What's next?

Step 3: Lower the hurdles

Orienting Question: *What are the most persuasive arguments I can make to address the concerns of my audience?*

The speaker was now in a position to begin creating his presentation. The concerns in Step 2 represented the outline of what he needed to persuasively address if he was to successfully sell his proposal.

The diligence needed with this step cannot be overstated. It is equal to the diligence needed in Step 2, and often requires even more work than we've already done to address particularly complex or troublesome interests and concerns. In this example the speaker needed to do a good deal of research to effectively address the last two concerns of his audience, about resistance and morale. In addition to focus groups and a survey, he did some research with other firms that had tried his hoteling approach.

A key takeaway here is that important concerns should never be finessed. Our audience won't be fooled. We must be able to address them head-on or admit that the time might not be right to move forward following our original plan. We may have to do more homework or break our original idea into more bite-size chunks, moving serially to our final objective.

Steps 4 and 5: Compose and Refine your message

These steps involve linking the message elements (defined in Step 2 and persuasively addressed in Step 3) in a narrative that is interesting and easy for the audience to understand and follow. In our example, the concerns from Step 2 group logically into four areas:

1. Why does this problem need attention now?
2. How can the problem be solved?
3. How much disruption will the change cause and how will we manage it?
4. What are the next steps?

Here is one possible outline for the presentation.

- Open: *Good morning, and thank you for being here. I'm going to spend the next fifteen minutes or so talking with you about reducing the amount of office space we lease and getting your agreement to move forward with the next steps in the downsizing process.*
- Problem: *I know we've all talked about this informally, but in the interest of common understanding, I'll start by briefly highlighting how we use our office space today and how this points to a reduction in the amount of office space we should lease tomorrow. Today, we have "x" square feet of space under lease...*

Here's where we...
  - describe important facts about office space utilization.
  - present simple diagrams or charts showing the low occupancy per square foot of space.
  - make the case that most of the office space is empty most of the time and that significant savings can be realized by changing the way the space is used.
  - use PowerPoint to keep our message clear, simple, and complete.

- Alternative: *Now let's look at an alternative. This comes from studying what other firms in situations similar to ours have done to use their office space more efficiently. As you know from our informal discussions, the alternative is office hoteling...*

Here's where we...
  - briefly review how hoteling works, how much space and money it would save, and its pluses and minuses. The descriptions must be clear, crisp, and concise.

- briefly discuss hoteling alternatives if appropriate to the audience. In this case it was not, since the informal background work prior to the presentation had focused the audience on the hoteling option, but only at a conceptual level.

- Issues and Actions: *I'd like to spend the next few minutes talking about resistance to the hoteling alternative—how much we can expect, what effect it could have, and what we can do to get people on board. Based on our work with focus groups, a survey, and the experience at other firms...*

Here's where we...
- identify the potential issues hoteling could create and discuss the work done to uncover and address them. Issues and concerns must be from the point of view of the audience. What are they concerned with and how can those concerns be addressed? Do a thorough job of uncovering all the issues and be candid in addressing them.
- keep this at the plan level and use no more detail than necessary to support the arguments.

- Next Steps: *So, what's next? Here's a high level look at the next steps we can take now to move this forward.*

Here's where we...
- present "next step" charts, using PowerPoint. Be careful—this is often where far too much detail is put into the presentation. Keep it high-level and readable; the audience needs to know the overall plan first.

Example B: A request for rezoning

This presentation started out with the speaker wanting the zoning board to recommend to the county commission that a ten acre parcel of property be rezoned for multiple family dwellings. The parcel was contiguous with two hundred acres that were being developed for single family dwellings.

Step 1: Say what you want
Orienting Question: *What do I want my audience (of one or many) to think or do differently as a result of my message?*

Unlike Example A, the answer to this Step 1 question was crystal clear. The speaker wanted the zoning board to recommend to the county commission that the ten acre parcel be rezoned for multiple family dwellings. Even with such clarity, however, it was important to pursue the *why* and *how*. Although the *why* was not particularly helpful, the *how* provided a specific plan for the way the rezoned land would be used, taking the audience from the general conceptual level (multiple family dwellings whose density they objected to) to where those dwellings would be, how many there would be, how they would be positioned relative to one another, and what they would look like.

As we will see, a visual representation of the *how* served as the speaker's principal argument in favor of the rezoning request.

Step 2: List the hurdles
Orienting Question: *What are the most important interests, issues, questions, concerns, or fears that my audience has that will prevent me from getting what I want?*

In this example this answer was also easy. An early written submission to the zoning board had resulted in a written response from the board's technical expert saying he would be recommending against the rezoning request based on the building density of the proposed land. The speaker was welcome to present his proposal at the next zoning board meeting, but the county had a restriction on homes per acre, which the speaker's multi-family proposal exceeded. This was the sole reason given for recommending denial of the rezoning request.

Step 3: Lower the hurdles

Orienting Question: *What are the most persuasive arguments I can make to address each and every concern of my audience?*

This is where the current example got tricky. The only objection to the rezoning request, housing density, was also the one that would stop it in its tracks. The problem was that a proposal that met the county's density restrictions would not produce the financial returns to make developing the land worthwhile, since, in effect, the restrictions prohibited townhome (multiple family) developments. If the speaker couldn't sell his proposal, the project would not move forward.

The persuasive argument for this example turned out to be much more visual than narrative. It centered on three large, colored architectural renderings. One was an aerial view illustrating the ten acre town home development, another was an aerial view of the two hundred acre development that the ten acres would be integrated into, and the third was a compilation of photographs and conceptual drawings showing how the natural features of the ten acres would be enhanced as part of the development project.

The presentation strategy was to help the county justify breaking its own density restrictions based on sensible land use. The intent was to demonstrate that the spirit of the law was well served even if the letter of the law was not, using the following rationale:

Density: The proposed ten acre development had townhomes placed on slightly less than half of the ten acre parcel, making the development appear mathematically more dense on paper than it would appear visually (although density for the ten acre parcel still exceeded county restrictions). The reason for using only half the acreage for dwellings was to preserve and enhance the natural features of the land and create a small pocket park with wooded walking trails for residents to enjoy. It is important to note that the aerial view of the proposed development was striking in its apparent lack of housing density. In other words, when looking at the illustration, it was very difficult to see it as densely built, though the dwellings were townhomes and the calculations clearly exceeded the county density restrictions, since they were calculated on a per-acre basis.

Sensible Land Use: The proposed ten acre development integrated sensibly into the existing two hundred acre development, sitting adjacent to a commercially zoned shopping area to the west, and the smaller properties of the two hundred acre development to the east. With eastward movement into the two hundred acre development, properties got larger, ending with some five acre parcels on the far east side of the development. What's more, the entire development had an equestrian theme, which seamlessly continued into the ten acre parcel with proposed horse and walking trails.

Land Preservation: Residential development of the ten acres would preserve the natural features of the land, which was being eroded by unauthorized all-terrain vehicles.

Steps 4 and 5: Compose and Refine your message

This was a short but formal presentation before the county zoning board. The speaker used two large easels to support the three architectural renderings. One easel supported the rendering of the proposed development of the ten acre parcel and was always in full view since it made a visual argument that the land was not densely built.

The second easel supported the other two renderings, one showing the two hundred acre development and the other the natural feature enhancements. These were set one behind the other and would be shown one-at-a-time to support the sensible land use argument.

Open: *Good evening. My name is John Smith and I represent ABC Associates. I'm here to talk with you about our rezoning request* (including the necessary identifying technical information).

Density: *I'll start my presentation this evening talking about the density of our proposed development, since I know that's foremost on your minds. In looking at this rendering of the proposed development...* This is where the speaker walked the zoning board members through the plan for developing the ten acres, highlighting how dwellings were situated on only half of the land to provide for openness, the park, walking trails, and the preservation of natural features.

Sensible Land Use: *I would like to turn now to how our proposed development fits into the broader architectural concept for the adjacent two hundred acres...* Here, the speaker turned to the other easel and outlined the argument that the proposed ten acre development was perfectly situated on the site, sitting between commercial and more densely developed residential properties. He also highlighted continuity with the equestrian theme and the natural features and park that all homeowners across the entire development could use and enjoy.

Land Preservation: *Before finishing, I would like to spend a moment illustrating how our proposed development protects and enhances the delicate natural features of this parcel, which are being slowly destroyed by the unauthorized use of all terrain vehicles, despite the county's best efforts to stop this...* (A stream, small waterfall, some rock outcroppings, and natural vegetation were endangered). The speaker moved the third rendering to the front of the second easel and showed, in detail, what was happening to the these natural environmental features and how his proposal protected and enhanced them.

Notice that the key to this presentation was confronting the density issue head-on. There was no attempt to make it less conspicuous by burying it in the presentation, treating it as one of many issues to be dealt with, or trying to persuade the county that density was really not an issue if it was calculated differently. The argument, instead, rested solely on helping the zoning board reach a conclusion that this was a good use of the land—maybe the best they could hope for—and that the proposal met the spirit, if not the letter, of the law.

Example C: Obtaining financing for a technology initiative

This final example is one of the most common in business: Obtaining financing for a project. Although the example is not especially complex, it does illustrate some common pitfalls in developing effective messages and how using the Message Architecture™ model can help avoid them. The example is from the paper industry.

Step 1: Say what you want
Orienting Question: *What do I want my audience (of one or many) to think or do differently as a result of my message?*

The speaker first answered this question by saying he wanted management to appreciate vapor recompression technology, a complex process used to separate very small solids from the liquid in which they are suspended. The speaker's answer, of course, begs the question: why does he want management to appreciate this technology?

His answer was that management would be more likely to use the technology if they appreciated what it could do.

This illustrates a common problem, especially prevalent in technical proposals and presentations: too much focus on often very detailed technical understanding at the expense of the business case. This is analogous to asking someone for the time of day and ending up with something like: *I'm happy to give you the time of day, but before I do, it's important for you to appreciate that the time I will be giving you will be the correct time. And that goes directly to the time piece itself. Now, let's talk about the time piece. The reason the time piece produces the correct time is because of high quality in the manufacturing process. Here's how that high quality is ensured...* and on and on. Don't do that to your audience. They don't need all the stage setting, especially before you give them the time. Tell them what time it is first. If they question your answer, you can then bring in more detail.

Resolving *what* the speaker ultimately wanted in this example was relatively easy, once the appreciation of the vapor recompression technology (*how*) was separated from the appreciation of the business value of the technology. What the speaker really wanted was $1.3 million to fund the vapor recompression initiative. As in Example A, clarifying who would be in the audience provided some initial direction for what they might be interested in. The audience consisted of the global finance team and the local executive team, a group principally interested in evaluating the merits of the business case. The technology could be examined more deeply by others if the business case pointed to moving ahead with it.

Turning to the question of *why* the speaker wanted to fund the technology project revealed that it could add a million dollars to the company's bottom line, year in and year out, through cost savings. So the end game in this example was keeping a million more dollars in revenue every year. The *how* was vapor recompression technology.

Step 2: List the hurdles

Orienting Question: *What are the most important interests, issues, questions, concerns, or fears that my audience has that will prevent me from getting what I want?*

Many of the concerns that needed attention in this example are common when funding is the objective. Care must still be taken, however, to ensure that all audience concerns are uncovered and addressed. The core concerns this speaker needed to deal with were:

- What is vapor recompression and why should we use it?
- How much will the project cost?
- How long is the payback?
- Why should we do it now?
- How long will it take?
- How much will the project disrupt our day-to-day operations?
- What are the risks and how will you deal with them?
- What are the ongoing requirements and costs?

Step 3: Lower the hurdles

Orienting Question: *What are the most persuasive arguments I can make to address each and every concern of my audience?*

As with the previous examples, the message begins to take shape here, with the speaker addressing each concern identified in Step 2. In this example we can conveniently group the concerns as:

- The technology: What it is and what it can do
- Financial: How much it will cost, the payback period, and why it should be done now
- Implementation: How long it will take to complete, how disruptive it will be, associated risks, and how they will be addressed
- Maintenance: Initial and ongoing maintenance requirements

Steps 4 and 5: Compose and Refine your message

Here is an outline of a presentation that worked well with this example.

Open: *Good morning everyone and thank you for being here. I'm going to spend the next few minutes talking with you about a way to put an incremental million dollars on our bottom line, year in and year out, without much investment and without much risk. We can do this by using a relatively new technology called vapor recompression, which allows us to take a giant step in improving mill efficiency and paper quality. Here's how...*

The Technology: *Today we haul a considerable amount of particulate matter—or muck—to landfills as a by-product of making paper, and we pay a heavy price for doing it. The reason we do it is because we've been unable to separate the components that make up the muck—silt-like particles suspended in liquid—and must dispose of the whole mess. Vapor recompression changes the game. It enables us to completely separate the silt-like particles from the liquid. The result is pure water for reuse in the paper making process and a solid, which we believe can be used as glue in the downstream converting operation. And the muck disappears in the process.*

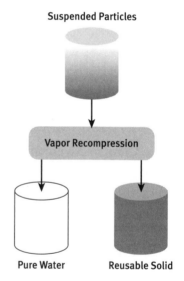

This was a good opportunity to use a simple visual. The visual could consist of a container of the actual muck along with a bottle of pure water and a container of the solid, demonstrating the separation that vapor recompression enables, or a PowerPoint slide with a simple illustrative diagram. The key was to keep it simple.

Financial: *There is, of course, an investment to do this. It's $1.3 million, which funds a six month, turn-key implementation.* Here the financials were discussed in a very clear and simple way with a sample slide to help structure the financial discussion:

Annual Return and Payback	
Reduce Disposal Costs	$200,000
Increase Paper Quality	$362,000
Decrease Rework	$380,000
Decrease Chemical Costs	$114,000
Annual Return	$1,056,000
Payback ($1,300,000 Project Cost ÷ $1,056,000)	1.2 Years

In this slide each area of return is discussed. Here's a brief illustration: *While you can see that disposal costs are significant, they do not produce the biggest return on investment by far. Increasing quality and decreasing rework do, and they are significant beyond the dollars represented here. As we all know, consistent high quality is a key reason customers choose us over our competition. So any reasonable action we can take to ensure consistent quality also helps improve our market position and our longevity.* Each area of return should be similarly discussed, keeping it simple, conversational, and straightforward.

Implementation: *I'd like to speak to implementation issues next, especially the potential for risk in disrupting mill operations.* As in our first presentation example, it was critical that all the issues be uncovered, including those the audience might not have thought much about. Candor was equally important in dealing with them. The case for dealing with risk in this example was made through operational history, emphasizing three previous successful extensions of this technology.

Maintenance: *Last, but certainly not least, are issues of system maintenance.* Here, high level action items were identified.

Approval to Move Forward: If enough behind-the-scenes work has been done before the presentation, this is the place to ask for approval to move forward. If that request turns out to be inappropriate here, then this is the place to clearly identify next steps to getting approval. The decision about what you want from the audience, however, should be made before the presentation and changed only if something in the presentation indicates more work needs to be done.

Delivery Tips

Whether you are giving a formal presentation or speaking casually one-on-one, these thirteen tips will always improve your delivery and the power of your message.

1. **Make eye contact.** Eye contact is how we engage one another. We look for it whenever people are speaking with us and we become suspicious of them when they don't look into our eyes. We often interpret the avoidance of eye contact as insecurity, a lack of confidence, or someone not being entirely forthcoming with us. So make eye contact with your audience. A good technique in presentation situations, or whenever you have multiple parties in a discussion, is to begin and finish a thought or two while looking at a single person, then repeat this with another person, and so on. With a little practice this

becomes easy and it will make your audience members feel like you are talking with each one of them.

2. **Smile.** A genuine smile conveys warmth, approachability, and a relaxed demeanor. While a smile is not appropriate in every situation, it's a safe bet in most. Do your best to use a genuine smile, even if it is not natural for you.

3. **Breathe properly.** This means breathing from your diaphragm. If you want a full, authoritative voice, you must push air across your larynx. Taking a full breath enables this. Nervous tension frequently gets in the way, resulting in shallow breathing and poor posture, which can constrict your airways (especially when sitting).

4. **Speak slowly.** If you want maximum authority and influence when you speak, don't rush or speak fast. Take your time and be rhythmic with your pace. Good ideas and important information should not be rushed.

5. **Keep your word count low.** Don't use extra words or filler words (*um*, *ah*, *you know*, *okay*, etc.). A high word count clutters and drains power from your message. Use only as many words as you need to persuasively make your point. And don't go on longer than necessary when making a point. Do it clearly and persuasively, then move on. Coupling a low word count with slow, rhythmic, and inflective speech, including pauses, will dramatically empower your delivery.

6. **Don't fade out.** Lowering your vocal volume substantially at the end of sentences is annoying to the audience because they must strain to hear you. If you make them work too hard to stay with you they are likely to tune you out instead. If you are

doing this—and you probably won't know until some brave soul points it out—break the habit. It's not that hard to do once you are aware of it.

7. **Use pauses.** Pausing is one of the most important and underused speaking techniques at your disposal. It can be used in a number of ways. Pause briefly, for example, to clear the air before starting a new idea. Or take a longer pause to focus audience attention, which is almost mandatory if you are asking them to think about something. Here's an example: *There is something I would like you to think about...* (pause). *It's an excellent example of what we've been talking about today...* (pause). *This is a proposal to...* Pausing always ups the impact of what you have to say when used intentionally and judiciously. The next time you're listening to a powerful speaker, listen for the pauses.

8. **Keep your body positions open.** Don't let your body be a barrier between you and your audience. Crossed arms and tightly clasped hands are good examples of closed body positions. Using both hands to hold an object is another. In addition to the psychological barrier closed positions create, they limit your ability to move in a relaxed way and to gesture. They can also convey nervousness or a lack of confidence to the audience, and make you feel more nervous at the same time. Rubbing your hands together while clasping them intensifies this.

9. **Gesture.** Use gestures to help your audience follow you visually. They can be very effective in underscoring your points and supporting the rhythmic flow of your message. If you are standing when speaking, remember to bring your gestures back to a neutral position, arms at your sides for example,

before your next gesture. If you are sitting while speaking, keep your forearms and elbows off the table when gesturing. Otherwise your gestures will lack energy and look weak. Keeping your gestures off the table will also force you to sit up and move slightly forward or backward in your chair, giving you a stronger, more self-supporting posture. People often ask what to do with their hands when they are not gesturing. The best answer is to let them hang at your side if you are standing, or simply place them in front of you in a relaxed way if you are sitting. Hands at your sides when standing may not feel comfortable at first, but you will grow accustomed to it and learn that it is a natural and powerful position.

10. **Never speak to a slide.** If you are using slides to support your presentation, don't look at the slides when you speak. If you need to look at a slide, stop speaking while you do it. Start speaking again when you are facing the audience. Speaking while looking at slides will drain power from your presentation. The slides become the audience and the audience members become bystanders.

11. **Move when you speak, but have a purpose and destination.** When you are speaking, too much movement can be distracting to your audience. Unless you have a purpose for moving and a clear destination, stand still but not stiff, with good posture and a relaxed bearing. You may want to incorporate movement by way of approaching or gesturing to an audience member to answer a question or to connect more directly; or you may need to move to address a prop or illustration. That's about all the movement you need. Pacing or wandering aimlessly will eventually distract your audience from your presentation.

12. **Acknowledge others.** Acknowledge the ideas of others with eye inflection and head nods. This helps you connect with your audience and lets them know you are processing what they have to say. It is also where pausing can play a role. If someone asks a question, use body language to affirm that you heard them and then pause, thoughtfully, before answering. But be mindful of the messages you can send when doing this, because negative acknowledgment (whether conscious or not) can convey disagreement or disgust, which will never help win an argument or win over an opponent.

13. **Never—ever—become defensive.** Defensiveness is a loser's game. It will weaken the strongest argument and erode support for you, even from those who are in your corner. Never use a sharp or whiny tone of voice; avoid excuses, arguing, eye rolls, and finger pointing (literal and figurative); and don't try to win by pointing out *all* of your adversary's faults. If you are attacked or put in a corner, stay calm. Don't take it personally. Keep your emotional distance and avoid negative internal conversations. Focus on the issue, not the person, and respond calmly. It's not about winning or losing and it probably doesn't need to be resolved on the spot. For some terrific advice on how to handle tough encounters, there is no better book than *Crucial Conversations*.[17] In addition to helping us understand the dynamics of these encounters, the authors provide examples of conversations that did not go well and include alternative conversations that would have been far more effective. Take the time to study it.

---

17 *Crucial Conversations: Tools for Talking When Stakes are High*, by Patterson, Grenny, McMillan, and Switzler. New York: McGraw-Hill, 2002.

Creating and Delivering Executive Messages

Step 1: Say what you want

Write down what you want from your message in a simple, unambiguous statement. Do not start creating your message until you have done this.

Orienting question: What do you want your audience (of one or many) to think
or do differently as a result of your presentation?

Step 2: List the hurdles

Understand the interests, concerns, and objections of your audience. If you try
to sidestep or finesse these issues, your audience will think that you either do
not understand their interests (you are clueless) or that you cannot deal with
them (you are irrelevant). In either case, your message fails and you lose.

Orienting question: What do I need to address to get what I want?

Step 3: Lower the hurdles

Create the main components of your message (your argument) by persuasively
addressing all of the interests and concerns of your audience. Creatively construct your best evidence for each point you will address, then provide no more
detail than absolutely necessary. And remember that facts do not persuade!
Logical conclusions, artfully presented, do.

Orienting question: What is the most important supporting information I can
provide?

Step 4: Compose your message

Keep your message interesting and memorable by finding its natural "story."
Group the message elements in a way that makes the story flow and logically
ties your arguments together. When your story is easy to tell and has a natural
narrative quality, you are ready for the final step.

Step 5: Refine your message

Review and edit your message for simplicity. Make it as straightforward as you
can. Be sure your audience understands why they are there, what you want
from them, and why it's a good deal for them, using simple words and short
sentences. Do not stray from the elements that make up your story.

■

CHAPTER NINE
What You Can Do Now

■

This chapter is about action. The focus is on making what you've learned about executive presence work for you, so we'll offer advice here that will both shape and accelerate your development.

We'll start by looking at 360 feedback, which reveals how others see you: the pictures of you they create when they interpret your behavior as you interact with them. We'll discuss some of the requirements for getting candid feedback and how important this feedback is to your improvement efforts.

Another source of feedback we'll discuss is video and audio analysis, which enables you to see and hear yourself as others see and hear you. While this can be challenging, since what you see and hear is often not what you imagined it would be, it is an essential tool in the most successful development efforts.

We'll finish the chapter with a discussion and some examples of how to use this information to create an Executive Presence Development Plan, concluding with some things to keep in mind to get the most out of it.

Get Feedback from Others

Understanding how you come across to others from their point of view is essential to improving your executive presence. You may know the leadership strengths and challenges of your behavioral style, but until you get critical, real-world feedback from others you won't have a useful picture of the behaviors you are projecting. Fortunately, honest feedback is not that hard to get, and only requires two criteria: 1) anonymity and 2) focusing the attention of feedback providers on the kind of information you want.

Anonymity

Without anonymity, the quality of the information you get goes down dramatically. No one wants to be critical to another's face; it is uncomfortable and can even be threatening (e.g., when the person requesting feedback has more power than the person providing it). People must have the opportunity to anonymously say what they think. This is why 360 surveys are so important. They provide confidential information you are unlikely to get in any other way. When properly done they directly reveal how you come across to others from their point of view. These surveys also provide information from a variety of perspectives as they reveal the thoughts of those who report to you, those you report to, and your colleagues (those with no reporting relationship). It can be very helpful to see the differences in the ways you come across to colleagues versus direct reports or bosses.[18]

Occasionally I hear concern that anonymous surveys make a "human dart board" out of the subject, incurring the unwarranted accumulated organizational frustration and discontent of subordinates and colleagues. In practice this rarely happens. There may be the occasional outlier with a dislike or vendetta for the person being evaluated, but most people err on the side of being too cautious or forgiving. If there is something in the behavior of the person being evaluated that is causing concern, a consensus about that behavior will tend to both validate the issue and flush out any revenge- or agenda-motivated (anonymous) reviewers. A well-constructed survey will help you find a behavioral pattern and determine what it is about your behavior that is creating the concern.[19]

Focusing Attention

To get the self-improvement information you need, focus your reviewers on the specific things you need to know. If you want to learn about the effectiveness of your executive presence, then focus them on any issues that are limiting your expression of executive presence—in other words, how they assess you on the Nine Expressive Dimensions. Although there are a number of 360 surveys on the market that can help deepen your understanding of yourself as a leader, they do not typically address the kinds of things you need to know to help improve your executive presence, at least not in a direct or comprehensive way.

---

18 A startling finding from recent research is that poor peer relationships account for almost 40% of executive failures. This underscores the importance of knowing how we connect with our colleagues—from their point of view.
19 This can be more difficult that it seems, since people are inclined to think, talk, and evaluate in terms of emotions rather than behavior. We must, however, identify the specific behaviors that are leading people to the conclusions they are making about us or we won't know how to change.

If you are relying on one or more of these surveys for help, review Chapters Three, Four, Five, and the Appendix with your survey results. See what the survey says about the issues discussed in these chapters, even if they are only indirectly addressed. If you are interested in feedback about how you come across to others and are attentive to what that feedback suggests, these chapter and Appendix resources will help you identify the kinds of things you need to work on.

Record Yourself

Another important resource that can help you identify what to work on, and how, are video and audio recordings of yourself interacting with others. These recordings provide a view of yourself that is impossible to get any other way. Without this resource you must rely on your imagination to assess how you come across to others, and your self-assessment may be very different from what others see and hear. The gap between what you expect to see and hear and then actually see and hear on the recordings is often surprising, and why this type of analysis is so important. Combining the insights gained from recording yourself with insights about your behavioral style and high quality feedback from others will give you all the information you need to begin changing your behavior in ways that can make a big difference in your executive presence. Here are two examples taken from my work with real clients.

> **Example 1:** Jake was vice president and general manager of a large manufacturing business and had done a masterful job of turning a money-losing operation around, yet he was viewed by his 360 respondents as lacking self-confidence. This feedback both confused and perplexed him, as it seemed so inconsistent with the decisions he had made

and actions he had taken. He didn't know what to do to turn these perceptions around. When reviewing his behavioral style analysis he appeared to be modestly assertive but not afraid to make a decision or take a stand, and yet his 360 results said the opposite. So what was the problem here? Why did his raters think he lacked self-confidence? A short videotaped interview with him revealed the problem, and he saw it immediately.

On the video, as he talked about how he had made the business successful, he was modest to a fault, using submissive vocal inflection, qualifying everything he said, beating around the bush, and using too many words to make his point. Based on this, Jake and I went to work creating more focused messages that he could deliver more directly and concisely. These and a few other subtle changes were noticed almost immediately by others in his organization and interpreted as an improvement in his self-confidence. Without video analysis as part of the assessment package, he would never have witnessed these problems firsthand or seen the relatively simple but disciplined and consistent correction needed to remedy them.

Example 2: A somewhat different but still typical example comes from Lisa, senior vice president of a large retail business. Effective throughout her career at getting results, she had a reputation as being very difficult to work with, which was preventing her from advancing further in the organization. Like Jake, Lisa was perplexed and frustrated by not knowing what to do to change these perceptions. Year after year she tried to do better, but every time the organization had her do a 360, her results showed little improvement.

In looking at Lisa's very forceful and assertive behavioral style and the comments about her behavior from the

Executive Presence 360, the problem appeared to be her inability to manage behavioral manifestations of impatience. Audio recordings of her interactions with direct reports and colleagues highlighted the behaviors that had created her "difficult to work with" reputation.

She began to make improvements that others could see by following a prescription of tactfully pausing before reacting (whether seconds, hours, or days), asking more questions, managing vocal inflection, not interrupting, and encouraging others to participate. Changing these behaviors, of course, created challenges with managing the emotions driving them, but working on both at the same time enabled her to make the steady, tangible progress that began to turn her reputation around.

An important note about these two examples, and countless others like them, is that my clients successfully improved their executive presence because they were able to isolate those few behaviors causing the unfavorable inferences and do daily work to change them. This focus on a small number of behaviors was essential.[20] Jake's behaviors involved message creation and delivery. Lisa's involved verbalizations that others saw as thoughtless and self-serving, which were driven by her impatience. Notice that there were no significant personality changes sought or produced in either case. Instead, there were subtle behavioral changes supported by better mastery of the underlying emotions. Although these changes were neither fundamental nor drastic, they were the most important things that Jake and Lisa could do to change the unwanted perceptions. The keys were isolating the behaviors, tending to the few that would make the biggest difference, then working diligently to make changes every day.

---

20 More than a few behaviors to work on is problematic for two reasons: 1) it usually means the source of the core problem has not been identified, and 2) working on more than a few things exhausts the client before any real change occurs.

Sometimes people are concerned with being transformed into something that is not genuinely them as a result of their executive presence improvement efforts. But this is almost impossible to do and is not the intent even if it could be done. The intent is simply to change habits of behavior in ways that create a more powerful, influential, and complete leadership persona.[21]

---

21 Excellent sources of help with getting in closer touch with our emotions and mastering them are *Working with Emotional Intelligence* by Daniel Goleman, Bantam Books, 1998, and *Decent People, Decent Company* by Robert and Carolyn Turknett, Davis-Black, 2005. Excellent sources of help with changing habits are *The Power of Habit* by Charles Duhigg, Random House, 2012, and *The Power of Focus* by Jack Canfield, Mark Victor Hansen, and Les Hewitt, Health Communications Inc., 2000.

Create Your Plan

Another key to successfully improving your executive presence is creating a simple, focused, and measurable, plan. The results for those who spend time planning are almost always better than for those who don't. A good plan will distill assessment results, provide direction, help with measurement, and keep your planned executive presence improvement actions in front of you every day. The Executive Presence Development Plan on the facing page is a template for the kind of plan we're talking about.

Here are some things to get you thinking about what you might do in your Development Plan...

Stop...	Start...
Providing too much information	Asking more questions
Relieving anxiety by talking	Being an active listener
Speaking fast	Encouraging others to participate
Being confrontational or harsh	Keeping the conversation focused
Assuming bad intent	Seeking feedback
Having negative internal conversations	Staying positive
Being judgmental	Being sensitive to others' needs
Being defensive	Being tactful
Being too intense	Limiting word count
Taking myself too seriously	Using a little humor
Trying too hard to please	Speaking up more
Taking things personally	Being more aware of my emotions
Being repetitive	Being silent more
Being silent	Acknowledging others' ideas
Dominating the conversation	Checking for understanding

Before starting your plan, or while creating it, you might find it helpful to look at the plans created by our travel partners, Diane, Blake, Melissa, and Andrew, especially the plan of the partner you most identify with. In addition to the plan, you will also see the rationale behind it, which can help you more effectively use the resources available to you. As you look at these plans, keep in mind that the travel partners created them and each plan reflects his or her unique issues and actions.

Executive Presence Development Plan

Dimensions Affected	Problem Behaviors

What I'm going to do...
Be specific with the behaviors, timing, measurements, feedback, and who will help

Diane

Diane knows from her Executive Presence 360[22] and other feedback she has received over the years that she has some challenges with her executive presence. From her 360 she knows that her impatience sometimes shows when she encounters obstacles. Most of her respondents said they were Somewhat Satisfied, Somewhat Dissatisfied, or Dissatisfied when asked to rate her calmness and reasonableness under pressure. Her raters also made several clarifying remarks about her being too passionate and too self-confident at times. This same level of dissatisfaction showed up again when the raters were asked to rate her openness to the views of others and her ability to confront the world as it is, with several clarifying remarks about her becoming so invested in an idea or project that she stops listening to suggestions for modification or course correction.

Although Diane was surprised by the number of people who found her lacking either skill or balance in expressing her challenging dimensions, she has known all along that these were problem areas for her. Her behavioral style report[23] provided additional confirmation by highlighting her very dominant and assertive style. Inherent in her style is a task focus and do-it-now approach that work against her slowing down and being more open, interested, and attentive to other points of view, especially when under pressure.

Now that it has all caught up with her, what is she going to do? Let's look at Diane's Executive Presence Development Plan.

---

22 This is a proprietary assessment instrument that asks others to rate the person being assessed on the expression of the Nine Expressive Dimensions.

23 This is from a DISC-based behavioral style analysis not discussed here. It is one of several additional tools recommended for improving self-awareness.

Diane's Executive Presence Development Plan

Dimensions Affected	Problem Behaviors
Poise: composure	Although rare, can be blunt, autocratic, and flippant
Self-confidence: overconfidence	Don't always appear to respect other points of view
Candor: seeing the world as it is	Sometimes closed to alternative ideas and actions
Openness	Occasionally have trouble admitting mistakes
Thoughtfulness: really am thoughtful but don't appear that way because of the issues above	

What I'm going to do...
Be specific with the behaviors, timing, measurements, feedback, and who will help

Walk slower and talk slower

Acknowledge to myself when I am becoming tense or emotional and STOP

Ask clarifying questions about competing views instead of immediately pointing out why they are wrong

STOP having negative conversations with myself when I disagree with someone, especially when it is emotionally charged

THINK about how I am going to say what I say BEFORE I start to say it.

Comments: From Diane's plan you can see that she is focusing on a few behaviors that will make a big difference. Asking clarifying questions before saying someone is wrong and consciously choosing the words and inflection she will use before speaking are actions that others will see and hear. But notice that Diane is acknowledging and trying to actively manage her emotions as well. Sensing when she is becoming tense or emotional and not having negative conversations with herself are two examples of this. The other, not-so-obvious example is walking and talking slower. Although both are clearly behavioral, they are in her plan because of their physiological effects. Slowing down our physical movements has a calming effect. For Diane, this will help her pull back a little on her assertive, do-it-now, approach, especially when she is under pressure.

Blake

Blake's Executive Presence 360 was unequivocal in highlighting two areas of opportunity for improving his executive presence: 1) tighter and more disciplined focus and follow-through with his initiatives, 2) being better organized and using fewer words to make his points.

This came out most clearly when respondents were asked about Blake's clarity. Most said they were Somewhat Dissatisfied or Dissatisfied, adding comments about the way he goes on too long and loses focus on key ideas. The loss of focus, in particular, was the subject of many remarks. Typical respondent comments were "put fewer balls in the air," "show stronger follow through," "needs to finish what he starts," "talk about things more directly and simply," and "stop talking when you have nothing new to add."

Another indicator of dissatisfaction with Blake's focus and follow-through were his thoughtfulness responses, which were mostly Somewhat Satisfied and Somewhat Dissatisfied. Clarifying comments pointed to his situational listening and limited availability, making it hard for others to know what to do, when to do it, or how well they were doing in meeting expectations.

But none of this is too surprising when we take into account Blake's behavioral style. His natural creative energy and interest in involving others constantly push him to "brainstorm" new ideas and initiate projects. For Blake, a slower and more analytical pace saps his energy. He has, however, come to the conclusion that he must be more disciplined in managing this behavior if he wants his best work to be effective and recognized.

Blake's Executive Presence Development Plan

Dimensions Affected	Problem Behaviors
Clarity: Focus and word count	*Talking too much and going on too long, clouding*
Thoughtfulness: Listening and availability	*my main points*
	Situational listening, sometimes failing to process
	what's said
	Keeping commitments to others, especially
	being late
	Considering potential pitfalls
	Probing or attending to troublesome details

What I'm going to do...
Be specific with the behaviors, timing, measurements, feedback, and who will help

Stop talking all the time – dominating conversations and being the center of attention

Ask at least two questions BEFORE making a declarative statement

Use the Message Architecture model for developing messages

Practice presentations, trying to take words out and not go on any longer than absolutely necessary –

err on the side of brevity

Write down all commitments

Create follow-up time lines and reminders (with admin help)

Comments: An important thing to notice about Blake's plan is how it focuses on several small behavioral changes that can make a big difference if done well and consistently. Not talking all the time, asking questions (and listening to the answers), and being more organized can move mountains in the opinions others form about us. This "tiny tweak" approach always underscores a good plan. Unfortunately, people often miss the importance of taking small steps. They pass over them in pursuit of some kind of groundbreaking transformational experience. But starting with little things is the way real transformation begins. It makes the changes doable without exhausting us, produces something measurable so we can hold ourselves accountable, and paves the way to incremental growth.

Melissa

Melissa knew she would have some leadership challenges once she was put in a senior leader role. She's not blind to the fact, for example, that her seemingly detached and data-driven style often masks the real energy and passion that fuels her efforts. She also knows that her style often causes her to miss out on painting bigger-picture, more persuasive messages that would help motivate others to action. What surprised her was how many people held these troublesome perceptions and the amount of trouble these perceptions could cause.

Looking at her 360 results she can now see the extent of dissatisfaction and exactly where it's focused. Respondent ratings in three areas stood out: optimism, warmth, and especially clarity, with ratings on all three statements about clarity (clear and to the point, sees the big picture without getting lost in details, speaks persuasively) lowest of all. Almost all responded Somewhat Dissatisfied or Dissatisfied to the three statements about clarity.

Melissa's natural behavioral style—her behavioral comfort zone—highlighted these vulnerabilities. Her task focus, detail orientation, and need to be right all push her messages toward data clutter and starchy stiffness, causing her relationships to be non-emotive.

Comments: Melissa's plan is narrowly focused on two things: 1) improving the creation and delivery of her messages and 2) engaging with others beyond the tasks they are working on. An important, albeit not obvious, element of Melissa's plan is leveraging the tight relationship between her guarded emotions and the resulting behaviors. The idea is that by gently pushing Melissa to show more

Melissa's Executive Presence Development Plan

Dimensions Affected	Problem Behaviors
Clarity: More big picture – less detail – more persuasion	Too much detail without a good organizing theme and narrative
Warmth: Approachability	Too matter of fact
	Don't engage emotionally with others

What I'm going to do...
Be specific with the behaviors, timing, measurements, feedback, and who will help

Use the Message Architecture model when developing messages

Create more persuasive narratives

Use more vocal inflection, pausing, and calmer pacing when speaking

Show an interest in others personally (beyond the task they are responsible for)

When evaluating ideas and proposed initiatives, find a positive for every negative

Engage a coach to help and identify a mentor in the organization for regular feedback

emotion (through gradually increasing her vocal inflection, gestures, pausing, and more rhythmic speaking), she will become more comfortable doing it, and actually become less emotionally guarded in the process.

Notice also that Melissa plans to work with a coach. When creating her plan she felt that working with a coach was essential for successfully reshaping the way she creates and delivers her messages (in any setting) and engages with others. She wanted a coach who could model the desired behavior, impose discipline on the change process, and provide video feedback from the coaching sessions. She also decided to find a trusted colleague in her organization to be her mentor, providing additional feedback and reinforcing her efforts.

Andrew

Nothing in Andrew's Executive Presence 360 really surprised him. He's heard for a long time that he needs to stand his ground more and let his voice (and ideas) be heard, and he knows that shying away from the spotlight and trying too hard to please have hurt his executive presence. Respondent dissatisfaction confirmed this and was clustered in two areas. The most dissatisfaction, by far, was with Andrew's self-confidence and decisiveness, where almost all respondents were Somewhat Dissatisfied or Dissatisfied. On being honest and forthright, most respondents ranged from Somewhat Satisfied to Dissatisfied, with the focus on Andrew's reluctance to say anything that might result in conflict or hurt feelings. Typical clarifying remarks were, "we need to hear his ideas more directly," "he needs to speak up when he disagrees," and "he needs to hold others to the same high standards he holds himself to."

As with our other travel companions, Andrew's behavioral style elucidates the source of his executive presence challenges. People-oriented and private by nature, Andrew is the consummate team player. Although task completion and accomplishment are important to him, his natural inclination is to first think about how a statement or proposed action will affect others. When this inclination is coupled with his aversion to confrontation and conflict, it is easy to see how the boldness others would like to see more of is outside his comfort zone.

Comments: Andrew's plan is another good example of the "tiny tweaks" approach. Here the tiny tweaks are a way to keep it safe, with behavioral changes that go just outside his comfort zone, but not very far outside. They stretch him but don't break him. Unlike

Andrew's Executive Presence Development Plan

Dimensions Affected	Problem Behaviors
Poise: Composure	Too tentative and self-effacing
Self-confidence: Not authoritative	Don't speak up and share ideas
Candor: Afraid to offend	Don't correct others directly enough or soon enough

What I'm going to do...
Be specific with the behaviors, timing, measurements, feedback, and who will help

Speak up at every staff meeting, even if it is to simply affirm or highlight the importance of someone's idea

Start to gently push back when someone rejects my ideas, using practiced phrases for doing this

Accept compliments with a "thank you" instead of a self-effacing remark

Stop qualifying everything I say

Use fewer words and more directness to make a point

Have corrective discussions with direct reports when an issue is first seen rather than letting things
 build up to possible confrontation and conflict

Diane, who needs to pull assertiveness boundaries in, Andrew needs to push his out—a little at a time.

Affirming someone's idea at a staff meeting and simply saying thank you when receiving a compliment are easy ways to begin. Gently pushing back by putting a rejected idea on the table again is a little more difficult, but using collaborative, non-confrontational phrases that he practices beforehand will make this easier for him.

Perhaps the hardest thing for Andrew in his plan is correcting others, which he has always been uncomfortable with and put off doing. But delaying corrective discussions only makes them more difficult, allowing feelings to fester and offenses to accumulate. Andrew plans to immediately talk about corrective action with his direct reports to reduce tension and facilitate smoother, more productive discussions.

Rules for Ongoing Improvement

Here are some important things to consider as you work on your executive presence.

Executive presence is a full-time job. You can't turn it on and off at will. If you want your expression of executive presence to be authentic, then it must be a true expression of you. That means that your executive presence is the same in every setting and in any company. It is the same in formal presentations and informal conversations; in writing, on the phone, and face-to-face; with colleagues, direct reports, family, and friends. It is your expression of the best you can be. You must commit to practicing these skills at all times.

Always communicate powerfully. Our audiences don't separate us from our messages so we must always communicate powerfully. Whether in informal, one-on-one conversation, a formal presentation, or a meeting, others come to know us by how we speak.

Be careful of the conversations you have with yourself. When these conversations disparage others because you feel disappointed or frustrated with something someone has said or done, such conversations will only inflame your emotions, justifying ill will and the often questionable behavior that accompanies it. Although you might feel righteous in the moment, that moment won't last long and the actions from it will do nothing but damage your executive presence.

Know your business. Make sure you understand the goals and direction of the business you are in. What are the cultural norms of your company and the characteristics of company leadership? How does the business make money? How does the business relate to the broader industry it is a part of. Know how you fit into the business and how your capabilities, interests, experience, and track record serve it.

Expand your personal network. Getting to know people inside and outside your organization will help your development and career progress. An important and interesting academic study on the practical importance of expanding personal networks found that those with many, less intense relationships (expanding acquaintances) fared much better at getting a new job than did those with fewer but more intense relationships (limited to close friends).

Find mentors. A mentor can help you navigate company politics and keep your balance in rough seas. With a mentor's guidance you can learn to keep situations in context, not take things too seriously, and see the bigger picture. The thing most executives say when asked about the path to their success is that they had good mentors and coaches along the way. These mentor relationships needn't be formal or intense and can simply grow out of a respect for the potential mentor's advice and their willingness to share it with you.

Work your plan every day. You will see results. Remember to keep it simple, behaviorally based, and up-to-date. And remember that it is important to recognize success and not get down on yourself when you're less than perfect. Just keep working at it with discipline and patience. You will be richly rewarded for your efforts.

What You Can Do Now

Get Feedback from Others

Understanding how we come across to others from their point of view is essential to improving our executive presence. To get good feedback it must be 1) anonymous and 2) focused on what we want to know.

Anonymity: We need anonymous feedback because people are reluctant to be critical of one another when face-to-face. It can be uncomfortable and even threatening (e.g., when the person requesting feedback has more power than the person providing it).

Focusing Attention: If we want to learn about our executive presence, then we must direct our reviewers' attention to any issues that are limiting our expression of it. We must get information about our skill and balance with the Nine Expressive Dimensions.

Record Yourself

Use video and audio recordings of yourself interacting with others to help identify what to work on and how. These recordings provide a view of yourself that is impossible to get any other way. Without these recordings you must rely on your imagination to assess how you come across to others, and your self-assessment may be very different from what others see and hear.

Create Your Plan

A key to successfully improving your executive presence is creating a simple, focused, measurable plan, targeting specific behavioral changes you will make. Those who spend time doing this planning always achieve better results than those who don't. A good plan will distill assessment results, provide direction, help with measurement, and keep your planned executive presence actions in front of you every day.

Rules for Ongoing Improvement

Remember, executive presence is a full-time job. Always communicate powerfully, be careful of the conversations you have with yourself, know your business, expand your personal network, find mentors—and work your plan every day. Keep it simple, behaviorally based, and up-to-date.

■

■

The Nine Expressive Dimensions

■

T he Nine Expressive Dimensions are provided here in outline form so you can quickly access their definitions, characteristics, expression, typical challenges, and associated universal leadership competencies when creating your Executive Presence Development Plan.

As we learned in Chapter Two, people with the best executive presence are skilled and balanced in projecting *all* nine dimensions. What's more, these people are seen as having outstanding leadership ability and/or future leadership potential, regardless of the extent of their content knowledge or job-specific skill. The Nine Expressive Dimensions are what define executive presence.

Passion

*Expressing focus and drive that show we are committed
to what we say and do*

Characteristics
- Must feel and express passion for something about the business and the job
- Cannot be faked—it is the furnace of commitment

Expression
- Strong vocal emphasis
- Emphatic gestures
- Significant variation in vocal volume, inflection, and rhythm
- Visible engagement—dressing the part and acting the part

Challenges
Does not feel passion for the work or the job
- In the wrong job or profession with little interest in the work
- Resists engaging for psychological reasons
- Is burned out or lacks the energy to truly commit
- Does not want to do what it takes to get ahead

Passion is felt but not shown
- Is not comfortable with emotional expression (relying instead on calm factual recitation)
- Does not know how to project emotional expression
- Does not know when to express emotion
- Does not think it is important to project emotional expression

Shows too much passion
- Is too spontaneous
- Displays too much energy, replacing clarity and focus with a general sense of excitement
- Is too enthusiastic; every exchange is a "pep rally"

Universal Leadership Competencies

Career Ambition: Has career goals and knows how abilities serve the needs of the business. Makes things happen for his/her self. Not waiting on others to identify opportunities.

Drive for Results: Consistently exceeds goals and strives to be a top performer. Pushes self and others to obtain tangible business results.

Perseverance: Displays energy, drive and the need to finish what he/she starts. Does not give up.

Personal Development: Strives to continually improve through learning experiences and feedback. Is actively engaged in the role and constantly looking for ways to enhance performance.

■

Poise

Projecting sophistication and composure that show we are comfortable in our surroundings and able to gracefully handle adversity

Characteristics
- Emotional maturity and self-control
- The ability to manage adversity
- Comfort in surroundings

Expression
- Measured, unhurried pace
- Knowledgeable and articulate
- Not tentative or defensive
- Relaxed in surroundings—the appearance of belonging

Challenges
Appears uncomfortable in surroundings
- Lacks familiarity with the environment (may be new to the organization or level)
- Does not know what is expected in the situation or encounter
- Has limited or no experience interacting with higher-ups
- Does not easily establish relationships with others

Is overly accommodating
- Tries too hard to please

Becomes defensive or argumentative under pressure
- Lacks emotional self-control
- Is not a good listener
- Does not understand how to produce win-win resolutions and/or lacks the skill to do it
- Uses sarcasm to show lack of agreement or lack of optimism in being able to produce a result

■

Reacts poorly to adversity
- Is too aggressive or too tentative
- Does not seek enough information about the situation
- Does not deal with the situation effectively

Lacks Sophistication
- Does not know social graces (manners)
- Does not know how to make social conversation
- Has limited worldly experience and knowledge, especially in higher circles

Universal Leadership Competencies

Composure: Remains calm under pressure and can be counted on in tough times. Keeps his/her balance when confronted with the unexpected. Is a settling influence and does not show frustration.

Comfort with Senior Management: Is not nervous or tense around senior people. Understands how senior people think and work. Approaches problems in a way senior people see as appropriate.

Conflict Management: Good at listening, reading situations, and resolving conflict. Good and finding common ground and win-win solutions.

Interpersonal Savvy: Relates well with all kinds of people, building constructive relationships. Is diplomatic and tactful with the ability to defuse tense situations.

Organizational Agility: Knows how organizations work and how to get things done in them, using both the formal and informal organizational structure. Understands the culture, politics, and reasoning influencing important organizational policies and practices.

Self-confidence

Displaying optimism and assurance that convinces others we have the personal resources and resolve to lead

Characteristics
- A sense of self-worth that is not based on position power
- A bias for action and the desire to initiate
- Realistic but optimistic about possibilities
- The courage to make decisions

Expression
- Short, direct, emphatic statements
- Pausing for emphasis with no unnecessary words
- Eye contact
- Moderate, steady volume
- Declaration of intention or position
- Initiating and doing

Challenges
Does not initiate action
- Needs too much evidence before taking action
- Is too risk averse to take action
- Is stuck in reactive mode
- Gives up too easily

Appears tentative
- Speaks too softly
- Uses too many words
- Does not use vocal inflection for emphasis
- Does not state positions clearly or support them well
- Is too concerned with what others may think or with the need to be liked
- Is too afraid of making a mistake

Does not demonstrate resolve
- Will not take a stand
- Changes positions too quickly
- Reacts to the moment
- Does not project a sense of urgency
- Acquiesces, allowing others to believe he/she agrees

Is too aggressive with others
- Tries to dominate
- Doesn't listen
- Interrupts and talks over others
- Demeans others
- Must always be in-charge; can't play on a team

Lacks flexibility (may reflect over-confidence or low self-confidence)
- Will not yield a point or position
- Always needs to be right
- Must have the last word

Universal Leadership Competencies

Action-Oriented: Initiates action and is energetic. Quickly acts on opportunities and sets challenging goals. Does not procrastinate.

Command Skills: Likes to lead and is not afraid to take unpopular stands. Encourages direct talk and honest debate of issues. Faces into adversity and gains energy from handling difficult challenges.

Dealing with Ambiguity: Is comfortable with change and can easily shift gears. Is not disturbed when things are not nailed down and is comfortable with moving on before completing the current task. Does not need to see the whole picture before taking action.

Personal Responsibility: Takes personal responsibility and can be counted on in tough times. Willing to champion an idea, initiative, or position. Comfortable working alone on difficult assignments.

Candor

Being honest and engaging with the world as it is,
even when it is not as we would like it to be

Characteristics
- Not afraid of the truth
- Honest and forthcoming
- Keeps commitments by walking the talk

Expression
- Not confrontational or argumentative
- Reasoned, not defensive
- Relaxed eye contact
- Measured pace with thoughtful physical and vocal inflection

Challenges
Hides from the truth
- Does not want to hear bad news
- Is afraid of bad news
- Tries to make situations less serious than they are
- Procrastinates

Is not forthcoming with others
- Avoids difficult issues that need attention
- Selects words that purposely confuse the issue (obfuscates)
- Hoards information
- Does not provide information in a timely manner
- Sacrifices candor to avoid conflict

Universal Leadership Competencies

Sharing Information: Readily provides information people need to do their jobs in a timely manner, regardless of the impact on him/her personally.

Personal Disclosure: Readily shares thoughts about personal challenges and limitations, admits mistakes, and is open about beliefs and feelings.

Honesty with Direct Reports: Reviews and openly discusses performance with direct reports on a regular basis. Deals with performance problems fairly but firmly and directly. Does not procrastinate when dealing with employee issues. Quickly and effectively deals with troublemakers.

■

Clarity

*Creating and delivering messages that others see as
crisp and compelling*

Characteristics
- Clear thinking
- Good message architecture
- Speaking and writing persuasively

Expression
- Messages that are resonant, interesting, and easy to follow
- Gestures, inflection, and pace that support the message (story)
- Talking—not telling

Potential Problems
Gets lost in detail
- Wants to tell people more than they want or need to know
- Does not prioritize or layer facts and evidence

Does not know what he/she wants from the message
- Is not clear on what he/she wants the audience to think or do differently as a result of hearing the message
- Lacks a big picture

Is not collaborative
- Is too concerned with telling, failing to draw the audience into the message
- Does not effectively use eye contact, vocal inflection, and gestures to engage the audience
- Jumps from thought to thought
- Talks too fast

■

Does not structure the message for the audience
- Fails to address audience interests
- Makes the message unnecessarily complex

Fails to use narratives
- Has not found the underlying story that makes the message interesting and persuasive

Universal Leadership Competencies

Presentation Skills: Effective across a variety of interactive settings (one-on-one, small groups, formal presentations). Can read an audience and command attention.

Written Communications: Writes clearly and concisely, getting messages across with the desired effect.

Managing Vision and Purpose: Communicates a compelling vision and sense of purpose. Rallies others to the vision. Inspires and motivates across the organization.

Openness

*Projecting a willingness to consider other viewpoints
without prejudging them*

Characteristics
- Active listening (checking for understanding)
- Sharing information
- Curiosity
- Not defensive

Expression
- Silence (listening)
- Asking questions
- Offering information
- Directly addressing concerns

Challenges
Not interested in new ideas
- Sticks with what is familiar even though it has stopped working or there may be a better way
- Rejects anything "Not Invented Here" (or by him/her), must always be his/her way

Mainly interested in what's wrong with a new idea
- Is not open to thinking about how a new idea could be used
- Unable to separate the idea from the person suggesting it

Threatened by unfamiliar situations
- Is too risk averse to seriously entertain new ways of thinking and doing
- Is afraid he/she will not be effective in the new situation

Unnerved by surprises
- Has trouble adjusting to change
- Resists change

Universal Leadership Competencies

Listening: Accurately listens with the patience to hear what others have to say. Can accurately restate the perspectives or positions of others, even when disagreeing with them.

Creativity: Connects previously unrelated ideas and offers new ideas and perspectives. Sees old situations in a new light.

Peer Relationships: Encourages a collaborative approach to problem solving. Seeks common ground and finds win-win solutions. Fairly represents self-interests and the interests of others.

Sincerity

Expressing conviction in what we say and do

Characteristics
- True to oneself
- Not just going through the motions

Expression
- Eye contact
- Affirmative head movement
- Soft vocal inflection
- Slow pace with pauses
- Attention to audience interests and concerns

Potential Problems

Ethics and values are situational
- Will do whatever is required to get the desired result
- Too easily swayed by the opinions or actions of others

Does not live the core values of the organization
- Too much of an individualist, doing things his/her own way
- Does not feel committed to the organization or have a sense of belonging

Doesn't walk the talk
- Says one thing and does another
- Pretends to support core values in public but does not follow through in private

May become cynical
- Expresses cynicism and sarcasm instead of being optimistic, supportive, or honestly questioning

Universal Leadership Competencies

Ethics and Values: Acts consistent with values. Doesn't abandon core values and beliefs during difficult times. Rewards behavior consistent with core values and corrects behavior that is inconsistent.

Fairness to Direct Reports: Treats direct reports fairly and equitably. Does not play favorites.

Thoughtfulness

Showing interest in others and concern for them

Characteristics
- Empathetic understanding
- Interest in the relationship
- Contributing through others
- Helping others

Expression
- Silence (empathetic listening) and affirmative head movement
- Questions
- Measured, unhurried responses
- Moderate voice volume (not emphatic)
- Soft inflection

Potential Problems
Impatient with others
- Does not try to understand issues or concerns others may have
- Talks over others
- Answers questions before they are completely asked
- Is intolerant of those slower to understand or get on board with ideas, plans, or programs

Appears self-centered
- Shows little interest in the opinions of others
- Appears distracted when talking with others
- Treats the opinions and agendas of others as secondary
- Does not think through issues before talking about them
- Focused on personal agenda
- Actions serve self-interest at the expense of team interest

Universal Leadership Competencies

Patience: Works to understand relevant information and the people involved before making judgments or taking action. Sensitive to processes, pace, and disagreement. Waits for others to catch up.

Compassion: Cares about others and is readily available to help them. Is sympathetic to those less fortunate and empathizes with the happiness and pain others feel.

Caring: Is interested in people beyond their functional utility. Asks about personal interests and goals and is available to listen and provide guidance.

Warmth

Being physically and emotionally accessible

Characteristics

- Approachable
- Caring
- Inclusive
- Reaching out

Expression

- Relaxed eye contact
- Smiling
- Relaxed, open positions
- Initiating dialog
- Affirmative gestures signaling openness and interest (head nods, arched eye brows)
- Soft, reassuring vocalization

Challenges

Uncomfortable with others through being either shy or arrogant

- May not acknowledge others
- Does not reach out to others or try to engage them in conversation
- Goes out of his/her way to avoid engaging with others

May see others primarily in functional terms

- More interested in tasks than people
- Not interested in entering into or deepening relationships

Universal Leadership Competencies

Approachability: Reaches out to others and puts them at ease. Is easy to engage with. Builds rapport with others through being interested, patient, and a good listener.

Humor: Can use humor to ease tension. Often makes him/herself the butt of a joke. Does not try to be funny at the expense of others.

■

The Executive Presence Workshop

Executive Presence – Making It Work for You is an engaging, informative, and practical two-day workshop that helps participants increase their comfort, confidence, and effectiveness when working at the executive level.

Here's a short sampling of what participants have to say about the lasting benefits of the workshop:

> *"A warm, supportive environment where it was safe to participate and learn. The content was clear and well sequenced. I walked away with a clear picture of the actions I want to take to improve my executive presence!"*

> *"Very interactive, comfortable, and interesting. The facilitators were absolutely fantastic."*

> *"The 360 exercise really opened my eyes. I now have focus and direction for improvement. ...the content, participation exercises, and class size were well balanced. Thanks!"*

> *"...tremendous opportunities for ongoing self-improvement. Both facilitators were amazing, talented, and warm. Loved them."*

> *"Good pace and well presented. The facilitators were knowledgeable and energetic. They keep you engaged! Thank you, fantastic job!"*

> *"I liked having and analyzing actual examples. The facilitator was very knowledgeable and very helpful on how to address problems—a wealth of knowledge."*

> *"Excellent! Great examples, use of media and other communication tools to aid learning."*

To learn more, please visit **www.executivepresence.com**.

■